Renegade Wisdom

A Life Guide

By

Bill Murray

Bill Murray
Renegade Wisdom

Bill Murray is now on his third career. Air Force officer, Novelist and Pilot Instructor for American Airlines. He is also5 the author of Renegade Colonel.

Bill Murray is on his third career. He wrote "Renegade Colonel" and has written his second book, and working on his third!

In his first career, he was an Air force Officer on active duty for 30 years. The first half of his Air force career, he flew F-111's and F-16's, and the second half of his career he was a Program Manger and Director for three large organizations including being the System Program Director (SPD) for the A-10 Program, and being the System Support Manager (SSM) for the all world -wide F-16's for Foreign Military Sales(FMS) supported by the US.

In his second career, for eight years he worked for Lockheed Martin as a Senior Systems Engineer on the F-22 Program, where he was the Life Cycle manger for that aircraft program. He then was put in charge of all advanced studies on the F-35 Program looking into bedding down that weapon system and improving the "stealthiest" and reliability of that fifth-generation aircraft.

In his third career, for the last 12 years he has worked for American Airline as a pilot instructor for the Boeing 757 and 767 aircraft. He was also selected to be on the initial cadre for the Airbus 319 and 321 aircraft. He is presently teaching General Subjects for all the aircraft-fleet pilots at American Airlines.

BOOKS BY BILL MURRAY

Renegade Wisdom

Renegade Colonel

Renegade Wisdom
Bill Murray

First Renegade Consulting LLC Paperback Edition

DECEMBER 2022

Copyright ©2022 by Bill Murray.

All Rights Reserved. Published in the United States of America by Renegade Consulting LLC.

This book is a work of fiction based entirely on the author's imagination. Any resemblance to actual persons is purely coincidental. Real places mentioned in the book are depicted fictionally and are not intended to portray actual times or places. All rights reserved. No part of this book may be reproduced in any form or by any means without the prior written consent of the author, excepting brief quotes used in reviews.

The Cataloging-in-Publication Data is on file at Library of Congress.

ISBN: 979-8-9868208-0-4

In accordance with the U.S. Copyright Act of 1976, the scanning, uploading, and electronic sharing of any part of this book without the permission of the publisher is unlawful piracy and theft of the author's intellectual property. If you would like to use material from the book (other than for review purposes), prior written permission must be obtained by contacting the author at billmurray75@verizon.net. Thank you for your support of the author's rights.

For my grandchildren

Luke (13), Kate (10) and Grant (7)

Dear Family & Friends,

It's January 2022, I'm 70 and I've begun to think about my life legacy and what I want to leave as my most important life lessons to my children and grandchildren and great-grandchildren. For many in this phase of their lives, as it is for me, it's a time of happiness and sorrow, as well as pride and regret. I've done many wonderful things, but also many, let's just say, "not-so-great" things. And I want to add with humor, as a guy who's getting older, "I'm not as good as I once was, but I'm as once good as I ever was!" I love that line from a good ole country song!

It's unfortunate that when we speak of inheritance or what we leave behind, we usually mean financial or material wealth. But leaving money and property is the easy part. The hard part is finding something of singular value that will help others, especially your family, lead a long, happy, and successful life. Thus, as I sit here and write these words, I now face the difficult challenge of trying to leave you, my beloved children and grandchildren an inheritance of greater worth.

To that end, I wrote this book. A collection of life lessons, pearls of wisdom if you will, that only time, experience, and God's amazing grace provide to anyone that's paying attention. Many of these lessons come from the *School of Hard Knocks*.

I have had to stand alone many times, and I've invited the opportunity to say and do what was right. I've been a renegade since birth. I was prevented from being promoted to Major in the Air Force when I had just been selected for the premier fighter weapons school in the F-111 community, because the Wing Commander had it in for me when he was trying to make his mark and I stood on principle. I got sent home early from a UN mission in Croatia when I was an Operations Officer, because I didn't believe in the tasking....we were risking American lives for nothing and I let my commander know it. I went up against executive leadership at Lockheed Martin when I thought they were taking advantage of tax payers, and I generally go against the flow when teaching, when I know we could do a better job with the curriculum and the delivery at any organization.

In the same vein if you are trying to put my theological perspective in this book into some category, box, or denomination like Catholic or Protestant or Evangelical, don't do it! Here's what I am....a follower of Jesus, a mere sheep, someone who knows the Master's voice, someone that doesn't have all the answers, a seeker, a friend of God, a Bible student, a life-time learner, a faithful husband, a loyal friend, and bottom line, a common ordinary sinner.

This is a book of philosophy and a book of truth as a result of standing alone and having three score plus ten years of varied life encounters all over the world. Many of you know from my first book, *Renegade Colonel*, my life is all about Faith, Family and Friends. This book is a personal collection of philosophies and truths based on those three principles and my street smarts.

I pass these truths along to Josh & Rosemary, Matt & Evelyn, Luke, Kate and Grant, as well as all other family members and friends fortunate enough to be born into, or associated with, the Murray Family, now and into future generations. I also hope this small book will attack believers and non-believers to examine how one can live a happier, more meaningful life. I sincerely hope these life lessons will help you, save you, and give you abundant life in the spaces of your successes, failures, trials, milestones, and life's highs and lows.

On the plus side of things many of you will probably be happy to know this book, unlike *Renegade Colonel*, will not be 700 pages! There are only five general principles I want to pass down to you. Children, I want you to learn them, think about them, and apply them to your lives as you grow and develop into strong men and women that please God and whom your Mother and I can be proud of......

This book is my love letter to you ~

Dad, Grandpa, and The Renegade Colonel

Jan 2023, Dallas, Texas

Foreword

So, here I am again, nearly 13 years later, writing another foreword to a Bill Murray book, with another "Renegade" title I mentioned in my foreword to Bill's first book, *Renegade Colonel*, how Bill and I met in the late 1990s when we were both assigned to the Air Force Materiel Command's Office of the Inspector General.

Somehow, we've managed to keep in touch over the years since we wore the uniform of the greatest Air Force of the greatest country in the world. Keeping in touch was made possible mostly because Bill would use his American Airlines perks to fly around the country, and when in the Dayton, Ohio, area would give me a call.

Many of us run into people during our lives that we sometimes refer to as "real characters." And that's the one thing I know about Bill that hasn't changed; he's still a real character. And I say that with the kindest intentions. The following story best describes what I mean.

I was heading home from a business trip and waiting for a connecting flight out of Dallas-Fort Worth Airport to Dayton. If airports were cities, the gates that service Dayton, always seem to be located in the seediest or most remote parts of airports. As I was sitting waiting for the flight to board, I noticed a figure walking down the concourse that looked familiar. As he came closer, I recognized it was none other than Bill Murray. It turned out Bill was flying to Dayton on the same flight.

About half way through the flight, Bill left his first-class seat to visit me in the cattle car. Bill had an American Airline badge hung around his neck which, from a distance, looked like the same ones worn by the flight attendants. As we were talking, the people around us couldn't help but overhear our conversation. Bill asked me if I needed anything. A young lady sitting next to me heard his question and asked Bill for some water.

Without missing a beat, Bill said, "Sure!" When he came back with the water, he asked if there was anything else she needed. I was laughing and the young lady was puzzled. I told her that he wasn't a flight attendant, that he actually was a flight instructor and probably trained the pilots who are flying our plane. The passengers who heard this started laughing and the young lady was embarrassed.

I tell that story because that was quintessential Bill Murray. Another person might have clarified who he was or called the real flight attendant over. But not Bill.

We tend to think that our monetary estate is the greatest gift we can leave our descendants. Pragmatically, I'm not naïve enough to argue otherwise, especially if the estate is a game changer. But for most of us, any estate we leave behind, after taxes, probate, and division among heirs, pales in comparison to the greatest gift we can give and that is our love reinforced though memories and conversations of our times together.

Renegade Colonel was an open book on Bill's life. The text that follows is an open book on Bill's faith – more specifically on what he wants others to know he deeply believes and wants to pass on to others. Although written primarily for his grandchildren, it contains important life lessons for us all. It is the greatest gift anyone can give.

George Bernard Shaw once said (paraphrasing), youth is too precious to waste on young people. It will be up to his grandchildren and those that follow for generations to come, to take this gift and cherish it, or mistakenly discard it for the next shiny gift box under the Christmas Tree.

Dr. Tony Corvo, USAF, Retired
Beavercreek, Ohio

A Note from Paul Hansen – My Lifetime Friend

Bill Murray defines the word friendship. It's been said that if a person has five good friends in his lifetime, they are truly a rich person. If you were fortunate enough to have Bill Murray as a friend, you were very blessed indeed. You might even say, you are rich in treasure and have won the lottery! There are many reasons this is true. First, Bill Murray will be a loyal friend for life. And you won't need to constantly make the effort to maintain the communication and friendship. Bill will provide all the energy and effort that is needed to be a true friend. That is because having and keeping great friends is one of the primary passions of Bill's life. And many, including myself, are very thankful it is one of his focused passions. Once you get to know Bill Murray, you will be shocked and amazed how many GOOD friends he has. But it is simply a matter of "Reaping what you sow." I've always told Bill that I am just thankful to be on his list of great friends!

Second, not only does loyalty and longevity define Bill's friendship and relationship with you, but maybe even more important and appreciated are that when you end up in a truly difficult spot, he will be present if he can. When everyone near you who you consider good friends seems to disappear in the woodwork, Bill will show up and be ready to help you get out of your tough spot. Many of us have experienced this wonderful friendship and know the type of help I am referring to. For me it happened when I had a brain hemorrhage and was left in a rehab facility and my Father had Alzheimer's disease. I was helpless and my family needed assistance in a bad way. When others were "busy" Bill flew up to Oregon and took care of our family for two weeks until he could spring me out of the rehab facility! That single act of kindness meant the world to me.

Third, Bill Murray is a giver and sharer. When he has good fortune, which seems to be often, he is always eager and ready to share God's blessings with others. This is obvious by the amount of time and effort that it took to write this book for you. To me this book reflects God's gracious abundance He has given to Bill, for his faithfulness over many decades.

Christian Fathers and Mothers are priceless. And if we have been blessed by God to have them, we have been blessed by God in a VERY big way. Jesus paid the price for us to receive an opportunity to be saved and receive an invitation into Heaven. In the same vein loving godly parents have paid a high price to teach us how we are to relate to God and what His expectations are for us. In this investment of time and energy, they many times teach us how to live meaningful, significant, productive, and successful lives.

Just like Bill and Judy's children, Rosemary and Evelyn, were blessed to have loving Christian parents, so were my brother and I. I'll focus my comments on my earthly father, Paul Hansen Sr. In describing my earthly father to a number of friends in different situations, I generally describe him as someone who truly loved. When he asked you how you were doing, he really wanted to know. He wasn't thinking about the next topic. His entire focus was on you and your life. He also was someone who wants to spend his life trying to make other people's lives better. This frequently meant giving up and sacrificing something he would have enjoyed doing or acquiring for himself. When our family began, we had very little in material goods and struggled like many of you. But even then, I saw my earthly father attempt to help other people get their businesses started in a successful manner. I could tell many stories about my earthly father, but I will end my comments simply by saying, "I know what it means to be truly loved" resulting in the sense that we really are important, valued, and mean something special to that person. What a godly example! Thank you Jesus for a wonderful earthly father! I think it is important to keep the focus on Jesus (giver) and not the gift (earthly father,) I am quite confident, he would agree.

Bill has graciously offered to let me add a few brief Life Lessons that I would like to emphasize:

1. OUR BIGGEST MISTAKE: Too many of us try to live life like the TV series "I dream of genie" where we rub a lantern and our every wish comes true. We do what we want, ignoring God until we get into trouble and need help or want something very badly. God may accommodate us a few times with the expectations that we anticipate, but once we have used up those first couple of wishes, He expects us to mature. Such behavior becomes unacceptable and will lead to unpleasant consequences.

2. WE MUST PAY ATTENTION: The God who created the entire universe loves us, gets jealous over us, and wants to spend time with us developing a relationship with Him. WOW! Incomprehensible if you think about it. God is calling us right now. God speaks to those willing to listen. Can you hear the phone ringing? Are you listening right now? We cannot live off someone else's relationship with Jesus. We MUST develop our own! And we MUST do our OWN HOMEWORK to become a mature disciple. My question is, "What is Jesus teaching you today?"

3. OUR CHOICE: Our percent of love and commitment is generally equal to our willingness to sacrifice for God.

We can choose to live our lives for Jesus and receive an invitation to spend eternity in Heaven, or we can choose to live for ourselves and be sentenced to hell for eternity, without the possibility of changing our destination.

Our commitment to Jesus is similar to a marriage relationship. Jesus made His choice, and He chose us. My final question for you is, "What choices are you making for Him and choosing for your final destination?"

A Note from Robert Hutchins

I was pleased to see that the auto-biographical **Renegade Colonel** has been followed with a sequel book of wise advice for parents and grandparents to consider as they "train up their children in the way they should go." Written in an easy to read and engaging style, Bill Murray shares decades of practical experiences from his solidly biblical worldview. Without any psychobabble agenda, he simply states the commonsense wisdom of the Holy Scriptures concerning the way we should walk and the way we should teach others to live a life that is pleasing to our Lord and Savior Jesus Christ.

After I left the Navy and was firmly established at a defense contractor, the Lord caused my path to cross with the man who would become one of my closest of friends for the remaining decades of my life. My wife, Nancy, and I had gone on one of our inexpensive dates and were walking out of Sears in a Dallas area shopping mall when a big fellow with an engaging smile came up to us and asked if I wanted to sign up to receive a Discover Card. I thanked him but declined, and we started to walk on. But he noticed my Academy ring, which for some inexplicable reason I was wearing that night, and asked me if I had gone to a Service Academy. A little bit taken aback I replied," Well, yes I graduated from the Naval Academy in 1975." He returned with, "I graduated from the Air Force Academy in 1975." Anyway, we started visiting and discovered that he was coming out to the defense contractor's location where I worked the next day for a job interview. He was hired, and we became close friends with Bill and his family, including Judy and daughters Rosemary and Evelyn. He became "Uncle Bill" to my children and their cousins - and no telling who else.

Later I discovered that Bill was working behind the scenes to get back into the Air Force, and he was ultimately successful at accomplishing that. He had been wronged and falsely accused in the Air Force effectively ruining his career, so he left the service. But after his appeal, he was reinstated with back pay and promotions and finished out his career as a full-bird Colonel.

Bill is a one-of-a-kind individual. After God made Bill, he broke the mold. I am not sure if the world could put up with, or deserve, another Bill Murray. Bill used to say things to me like, "There are two great guys in the world, and you're both of them." That was kind of corny, but he sure made me feel special. Being a friend of Bill's makes you feel like you are the most important person in the world and in his life. But he is not a flatterer. This simply flows from him as his big heart overflows with genuine caring, appreciation, and love for others. Dennis Swanberg, a self-proclaimed minister of encouragement, could have been describing Bill when he observed "the people we most admire in life often have a habit of self-forgetfulness. They are able to focus on others rather than themselves."

Bill is fearless in relationships. By that I mean

there was no person too prominent or influential to keep him from walking right up and introducing himself. To no surprise, he has many high-placed, influential close friends. And also, many non-descript, non-influential friends like me.

Bill is so outgoing and so outspoken that he takes a bit of getting used to. He has been an example to me of the way I could treat others for many years, if I could only get up the nerve to do so. Nancy loves

to tell this story about Bill when people need the snapshot of who he is. Bill worked in a program management office at E-Systems and had a particularly rough program status meeting one day. Later that day at a social event, he marched right up to the vice president

who was giving him a hard time in that status meeting and said, "Doctor Cates, good to see you again. I haven't seen you since you were yelling at me earlier today." What could anyone say to a person who was gutsy enough to greet you that way? I don't

think anything could intimidate Bill. When he was working at E-Systems, I considered hiring him into my department, because I knew how talented and capable he was. But then I thought about how I might kill him, or vice versa, if he worked for me. Ha!

I think he has been influential in my life because he is so different from me. I admire his nerve, fearlessness, outgoing personality, and his ability to resist being

intimidated by anybody, anytime, and any place. Bill genuinely cares for his friends, which is essentially everyone he meets, He also intensely loves his family, and I have always said if there were such a

thing as reincarnation, I would like to be reincarnated as one of Bill's children, or at least his dog.

Acknowledgements

When I wrote my first book, "Renegade Colonel" I edited it myself. What a mistake! When I had approved the final draft and the publisher put it into a hardback copy, I skimmed through it quickly and said to myself, "Who in the world did the editing on this! This is awful! There are obvious mistakes all over the place!" Well, as my mother would say, "Your book has personality!"

I'm happy to say, I didn't make that mistake this time. You see I am trainable! I just hope and pray that I got all their corrections in correctly! I am forever indebted to Dr Tony Corvo, who assisted me not only with editing, but in organizing this book. Gently he told me, "Bill, you can't have a book titled "Here are the 55 Most Important Lessons in Life You Must Remember!" His inputs in life, in his perspective about life, and in his editing my book have been invaluable.

I also want to thank Dr Bill Buchta, a medical doctor, classmate of mine from the Air Force Academy, and lifelong friend for helping me edit. After reading my first book, he gently said, "I hope you get someone to help you edit your next book", and then happily volunteered to help me! Bill is an amazing guy for many reasons, not only because he graduated in the Top Ten of our Class of 1975 (Best Alive), but also because immediately following graduation he got his Master's Degree from a prestigious university in six months in Psychology, and then preceded to re-write all the entrance exams for all the airmen entering the Air Force! After this assignment he was selected to teach Psychology at the Air Force Academy where he was bored, so he began to monitor Pre-Med classes of the senior cadets. Having an interest in Medical School, he took the MEDCATS (entrance exams to medical school) and almost aced them! Then he applied to various medical schools only to be rejected, because he had not been "enrolled" in certified undergraduate medical classes. In the end, he was accepted by a smart, but small medical school, where he graduated in the top of his class.......surprise, surprise! Today, he is a doctor for the Mayo Clinic in family practice. You couldn't find a better doctor, father or husband anywhere, or might I mention an editor who pays attention to every detail!

I would like to thank is a fellow American Airlines instructor friend of mine named Maurice Azurdia. Unlike me, Maurice is a real airline pilot! He flew for a number of years, and then was involved in a tragic accident where he was driving home after not sleeping for about three days, fell asleep at the wheel and drove off the road tumbling his truck over and over. As a result of this accident, he is paralyzed from the waist down! But let me hasten to say that he is the most optimistic, energetic, nice person you'll ever meet! He has written four non-fiction books and has a few others in the works. When I told him about my second book he said, "Please don't pay to publish it. Let me help you publish it electronically and get more coverage than you would from your previous book. Your book reminds me of that small book written by Admiral William H. McRaven titled "Make Your Bed" that has sold millions of copies! Let me help you publish this one!"

The last person I would like to thank is Rick Townsend, a fellow classmate from the Air Force Academy, Class of 1975 (Best Alive!), retired fighter pilot (F-15's) and Airline Pilot (Capt on the 737 and Airbus). Rick is a Christian who walks the walk, and can back up his positions with historical data and scripture. After retirement, he got his PhD in History of Ideas. It has always amazed me how much smarter my classmates were than I have ever been! They are Type 1 personalities, competitive on task, and never give up! He has really helped me push this final version across the finish line when communications and problems with Kindle came to a stand still. His superior Microsoft Word and Apple word processing skills were invaluable to professionally completing this document and making it look just right. He, like Maurice would take no money for their efforts, which were substantial! You can't find friends like these people!

I must say my ideas and life lessons were solid, but I just needed a little help from my friends! I always need help from my friends and God. That is how I have made it this far in life... another great life lesson!

Table of Contents

Foreword...iv

Acknowledgements xiv

Life Lesson #1 — Have Faith in God 1
   Your relationship with Jesus Christ 1
   Guidelines For Prayer 5
   God Speaks to Those Ready to Listen 9
   The Baseball Diamond Analogy 9
   The End will Come...12
   You will reap what you sow 15
   Follow God's Commands 16
   Honor Your Mother & Your Father 17

Life Lesson #2 — Family and Friends 20
   Get a Mentor...20
   Great Teachers 23
   Be careful who you trust...24
   Choose your Mate Wisely! 25
   Choose Your Friends Wisely! 43
   Drugs and Alcohol 51

Life Lesson #3 — Character — How to Live.........55
   Work hard 55
   Develop Personal Discipline 54
   Follow Your Passion...60
   Take care of Your Health..61
   Planning, Preparation and Execution 75
   Pay attention to the Details...................................76
   Pursue maturity...80
   When you do Wrong..80
   Don't follow the Crowd 81
   Be Responsible 84
   Take a lesson from the Marines............................88
   Be Teachable 91
   Be an Encourager! 92
   Be Proactive and Productive 92
   Self-Image...94

  Don't believe THE Press or YOUR Press 95
  Make Life Easy on Yourself.................................... 95

Life Lesson #4 — Your Attitude 101
  Think Critically 103
  Don't let emotion rule your life 107
  People remember how you made them feel.......... 112
  Don't be a complainer 113
  Adversity... 114
  Be Kind 117
  Smile 117
  Trials 118
  Finances and Learning to be Content 123
  Humility... 126
  Don't Be Afraid.. 128
  Anger 129

Life Lesson #5 — Entering into Maturity 132
  Pursue Genuine Manhood 132
  Some advice for Parents 133
  Running a family... 135
  Launch Your children... 136
  Buying a home 137
  Being a Success Professionally 138

Conclusion 141
  The Hard Truth 141
    Salvation Part I: Repentance and the race begins 149
    Salvation Part II: Learning to stay on the right path 151
    Salvation Part III: Entering the Kingdom 152

Have Faith in God – Life Lesson #1

Your relationship with Jesus Christ

When I consider what is most important in life, what is first and foremost, what is eternal, what is paramount, what is at the pinnacle of wisdom, only one thing comes to mind: Your relationship with Jesus Christ. Nothing else really matters or comes close in this life or the next. Christianity is relationship, not religion. The real question for everyone is, "What will you do with Jesus?"

This is my testimony. This is THE truth. We all desperately need Jesus in our hearts and minds. Real life is all about your personal relationship with the Living God. Nothing is more consequential in life. This is not religion. This is pure, unadulterated truth!

There is nothing more important than having this relationship with the living God established in your own life, and then being able to transmit that to your children. If you don't have this relationship, then you can't share it, so you can stop here on Life Lesson #1. But let me say: if you don't have it, there is still hope. You haven't missed the boat…the boat is still circling.

I don't want to sound high and mighty, but here's the truth. Jesus is God. He was the Son of God who came to earth in human form to experience what we do on earth as mere mortals. He came to set the ultimate example, to transmit ultimate truth in a few short years, to live and to die on a wooden cross, so that we would have the option, the personal choice, of ultimately of where we would spend eternity. We will all live forever. Jesus gave us the option to choose whether we would live with Him in heaven, or live in hell, forever tormented for our shortcomings, otherwise known as sin.

That is as simply as I can say it...... It's harsh, but these are not my rules. This is not my world. This is not my universe. God created the universe and He made up the rules both for living life on the earth and for eternity, which everyone will experience. You either establish a relationship of love, forgiveness, and grace with Jesus, or you choose to live a life here on earth without Him, and spend an eternity being punished for your unforgiven sins because you rejected Him and chose other gods.

God is an unchanging God. His character and his word are true. His promises have not changed since the time of Israel. He will never change. As He said in the Old Testament in Deuteronomy 30, Verse 19-20 *"Today I have given you the choice between life and death, between blessings and curses. Now I call on heaven and earth to witness the choice you make. Oh that you would choose life, so that you and your descendants might live! You can make this choice by loving the LORD your God, obeying him, and committing yourself firmly to him. This is the key to your life. And if you love and obey the LORD, you will live long in the land the LORD swore to give your ancestors Abraham, Isaac, and Jacob."*

But Jesus came not into this world to judge the world, but to save it.....to save you and me. He is the gentle Savior with high standards and complete integrity. He will never leave us or forsake us, if we are His true sheep. He is the Good Shepard. His is Light. He is Love. He is the Bread of Life.

He is all things good wrapped into one package. We must try to live our lives to please him, because He gave all……He gave His very life for us, not because He had to, but because He loved us. He freely laid down His life. We can trust Him implicitly even though sometimes the circumstances look out-of-control! He is trustworthy to the core and ever-faithful, even though we aren't faithful.

All you need is faith, and He gives that to you also, if you ask Him. In Ephesians 2:8,9 it says, "God saved you when you believed. And you can't take credit for this; it is a gift from God. Salvation is not a reward for the good things we have done, so none of us can boast about it. For we are God's masterpiece. He has created us anew in Christ Jesus, so we can do the good things He planned for us long ago."

Again, these aren't my ideas or my truth……this comes from Jesus who said, *"I am the way, the truth, and the life."* Either Jesus was a liar, or He was revealing a truth never before heard until He came to earth as a baby born to Mary and Joseph in Bethlehem. He only lived 33 years, yet He changed the course of the world forever with the help of His Father, the Holy Spirit, initially 12 motley men, and finally many disciples like me trying to teach these truths to their children and other people that Jesus serendipitously puts in our paths from time to time.

Everything else, however disjointed it may come out, are ideas and truth born of this relationship with God the Father, God the Son, and God the Holy Spirit……three in One, a hard to comprehend miracle. This One God in three parts or manifestations is known as the Holy Trinity.

The Apostle Paul in the first chapter of Colossians describes Jesus this way "Christ is the visible image of the invisible God. He existed before anything was created and is supreme over all creation", showing us that Jesus was present from the beginning of time, but he was made visible to all mankind when He was born of the Virgin Mary in Bethlehem."

For my many friends who don't know the Father, I pray that you will someday. It's my most sincere desire to live with you forever. You are on my mind and I love you with a Godly love. And God loves you and longs to have a relationship with you. Don't be afraid to start a faith journey. I am praying for you! Johanna Carlson, in her song, *You Belong to Me*, does a great job in expressing this thought:

> *But heaven is hearing and sharing each tear*
> *And I know the Father is near.*
> *He's saying you can belong to me*
> *I'll cherish you, treasure you, love you completely*
> *Someday you'll finally see how precious you are in*
>   *my eyes*
> *You've never been out of my sight*
> *I love you for all your life*
> *You belong to me*

If you don't understand any of the other lessons in this book, go back to this one and read the last chapter, "The Hard Truth" at the end of the book. They are the only life lessons that really matter. Everything else I've written is helpful, but not critical like these two chapters.

Guidelines For Prayer

When you pray, first of all think about who you are praying to. You are praying to the creator of the whole universe. God is ruler and creator of everything! No one can even measure His greatness. He is trustworthy to every promise. Nothing……no god, no person, no entity, nothing is above God. He is the First and the Last....The Alpha and The Omega!

The Apostle Paul tells us in Ephesians 1 that God is supreme above everything. In this first chapter he writes, "21 Now he is far above any ruler or authority or power or leader or anything else—not only in this world but also in the world to come. 22 God has put all things under the authority of Christ and has made him head over all things for the benefit of the church."

Further in Psalms 145 David writes,

> *3 Great is the LORD!*
> *He is most worthy of praise!*
> *No one can measure his greatness.*
> *13 For your kingdom is an everlasting kingdom.*
> *You rule throughout all generations."*

The LORD always keeps His promises; He is gracious in all He does.

Pray humbly and sincerely. Use your own words. Use memorized prayers. Pray the Lord's Prayer like Jesus said to do. Realize the name you are praying in is the Name above all Names, worthy of all glory and honor. Before you start asking for things you want, thank God for everything He is and everything He has blessed you with.......family, friends, and material possessions.

As you call out God's magnificent name, keep in mind of what the very word "God" means. This was posted on the internet.

There was a moment when Moses had asked God what his name is. God was gracious enough to answer, and the name he gave is recorded in the original Hebrew as YHWH. Over time we've arbitrarily added an "a" and an "e" in the name to get YaHWeH, presumably because we have a preference for vowels. But scholars and Rabis have noted that the letters YHWH represent breathing sounds, or aspirated consonants. When pronounced without intervening vowels, it actually sounds like breathing. YH (inhale): WH (exhale). So, a baby's first cry, his first breath, speaks the name of God. A deep sigh calls His name – or a groan or gasp that is too heavy for mere words. Even an atheist would speak His name unaware that their very breathe is giving constant acknowledgment to God. Likewise, a person leaves this earth with their last breath, when God's name is no longer filing their lungs.

When I can't utter anything else, my cry calling out His name. Being alive means I speak His name constantly. Is it heard the loudest when I'm the quietest? In sadness, we breathe heavy sighs. In joy, our lungs feel almost like they will burst. In fear we hold our breath and have to be told to breathe slowly to help us calm down. When we're about to do something hard, we take a deep breath to find our courage. When I think about it, breathing is giving him praise. Even in the hardest moments! This is so beautiful and fills me with emotion every time I grasp the thought. God chose to give himself a name that we can't help but speak every moment we're alive. All of us, always, everywhere……. Waking, sleeping, breathing, with the name of God on our lips.

We also find references in the Bible to support the sentiment above. In Psalms 150:6, we read, *"Let everything that breathes sing praises to the LORD!"*

Prayer is spiritual humility in action. We all need help. Pray regularly. Pray quietly. Pray privately. Get in your closet if you have to. Don't make a show of things, yet sometimes pray where others can see you and follow your good example. I always say, "Pray before meals so you don't choke!"

The Apostle Paul writes in the Book of Philemon, "6 And I am praying that you will put into action the generosity that comes from your faith as you understand and experience all the good things we have in Christ."

Where there is a lot of prayer, there are many blessings. Where there is little prayer, there are little blessings. Where there is no prayer, there are no blessings.

Padre Pio once wrote, "Be souls of prayer. Never tire of praying. It is what is essential. Prayer shakes the heart of God."

When you pray, ideally, pray where you can't be distracted, but pray everywhere at all times. Keep a good connection with God. Pray early in the day. Start your conversation with God when you wake up thanking for another day to live. End your day with prayer thanking Him for the day and laying your request at his feet.

The Apostle Paul was one of the most influential leaders of the early church. He played a crucial role in spreading the gospel during the first century, and his journeys took him throughout the Roman Empire. He writes in Colossians "4:2 *"Devote yourselves to prayer with an alert mind and a thankful heart."*

Sometimes, get on your knees. Humble yourself before the Creator of the universe. Bow your head in humbleness........Pray devoutly and fervently. Some people follow the practice summarized by the acrostic **ACTS**.

    A – Adoration
    C - Confession
    T - Thanksgiving
    S – Supplication

It is a good way and a good order to approach the Throne of God. Pray The Lord's Prayer. That is what

Jesus taught us to pray. Notice that The Lord's Prayer has all the attributes of the acrostic ACTS.

Billy Graham, my hero in the faith, said this about prayer:

> *"In the morning, prayer is the key that opens to us the treasures of God's mercies and blessings; in the evening, it is the key that shuts us up under His protection and safeguard."*
>
> *"True prayer is a way of life, not just for use in cases of emergency. Make it a habit, and when the need arises you will be in practice."*
>
> *"Have you ever said, 'Well, all we can do now is pray'? ... When we come to the end of ourselves, we come to the beginning of God."*
>
> *"Heaven is full of answers to prayer for which no one ever bothered to ask."*
>
> *"No matter how dark and hopeless a situation might seem, never stop praying."*
>
> *"Whether prayer changes our situation or not, one thing is certain: Prayer will change us!"*

God Speaks to Those Ready to Listen

Our search for God cannot be casual. He loves us and wants us so badly, but He will never impose His will on our hearts. As explained in Jeremiah, 29:13, *"And you shall seek me, and find me, when ye shall search for me with all your heart."*

Many people only seek God when they are in desperate need, when there is nowhere else to turn, or where no one else can provide the resources, the answer, or the healing. When only God can provide the answer to the need, that's when God shines brightest....... However, He is a jealous God. He wants all of our attention. He wants all of us all the time. If you are ready to listen, He is there. You've heard the saying, "If you can't find God, guess which one of you moved?" He is ever-present, constant and unchanging.

Sometimes God speaks to us through the Bible. The Bible is His Word, written by men, inspired by the Holy Spirit, and available in a variety of translations and formats. Some people say you can interpret the Bible in many ways. That might be true for some minor exceptions. But for the main message of God's love, grace, and salvation that He and He alone can offer, that is not true. The message of repent, be baptized and believe with your whole heart following in obedience, is repeated many times in many ways in scripture. That direction is very clear and easy to interpret.

As Paul writes in Colossians 2:12, "For you were buried with Christ when you were baptized. And with him you were raised to new life because you trusted the mighty power of God, who raised Christ from the dead."

Sometimes God speaks to us through different people. I'll never forget God started to talk to me through a Priest in Canada when I was an acolyte in junior high school. Father Large was the best. At funerals he would always be upbeat and say, "Well, Bill, we're sending another saint upstairs!" That made an impression on me! Listen to those you can trust. God later spoke to me at a Young Life meeting when I was a sophomore in high school. Then God spoke to me at a Fellowship of Christian Athletes Conference when I was a senior in high school. I was drawn to God and His people, because they had real love and no hidden motives. My initial concept of God I received from my earthy father was flawed. My true picture of the real God and His character came from a combination of things all mentioned above over a lifetime. He still speaks to me, sometimes loudly and sometimes in a whisper, sometimes directly and sometimes through my wife and children.

I hope the life messages in this book are speaking to you. I've talked to many people about the Lord. Some were ready to listen, and sometimes it just wasn't quite time for them to hear and receive the truth. Sometimes we need to hear a truth over and over to really get it. Sometimes it only takes once if you are ready and really listening.

Sometimes God speaks to us through circumstances, referred to as "God Moments" where something unusual happens that it's clear God is directing the orchestra! These events normally only happen a few times in life when God is trying to get your attention. Sometimes they are life and death situations. God will go to any means necessary to draw you to Himself. His mission is to redeem His people for Himself. As I said before, He is a jealous God.

God has many ways of communicating. He knows how to reach us. Sometimes God speaks to us out loud, other times through our hearts or in visions or dreams, but those are rare for most people.

God is always trying to communicate with us. However, we must train ourselves to not only listen for Him but also to obey; and obeying is often the most difficult. As Paul wrote in Colossians 2:6,7, *"And now, just as you accepted Christ Jesus as your Lord, you must continue to follow him. Let your roots grow down into him, and let your lives be built on him. Then your faith will grow strong in the truth you were taught, and you will overflow with thankfulness."*

Listen for God. Communicate with Him, and then trust and obey what He says. There's a little song I learned as a young kid in Sunday School that went, "Trust and

Obey, for there's no other way, to be happy in Jesus is to Trust and Obey!" That pretty much says it all!

The Baseball Diamond Analogy

Many times it helps us to visualize things. We are visual beings and this example of a baseball diamond will illustrate many of the points I've tried to make in the first Life Lessons.

Imagine a baseball diamond with a home plate and three bases. You hit the ball and you're running to first base......the first base of life. Here's what the bases and home plate might look like:

First base - You develop humility, gratitude and faith. You recognize, acknowledge and submit to Jesus' authority. You begin to develop a dependency on God. You honor God by learning His commandments and obeying them.

Second base - You learn personal discipline and responsibility. You deny yourself of temptations that surround you. You strive to please God and serve others, not yourself.

Shortstop - You develop courage and strengths for life's challenges

Third base - You develop perseverance and the long vision, not focusing on what is right in front of you. This is where you really learn to overcome adversity, knowing this is not your home.

Home Plate - You experience glory, because you have not taken the wide path, you have not chosen the easy road, you have not yielded continually to temptations and sin. You are an overcomer by God's Grace and He gets the glory and you've made a home run!

Albert Einstein once said, "Strive not to be a success, but rather to be of value."

The End will Come

As the old saying goes, "Only two things are for sure: death and taxes"! We are all temporal beings, but only God knows the number of our days.

When we are young, all we think about is our next birthday, being with friends, going to amusement parks, getting on social media or watching our favorite TV shows. When we get older, we think about dreams and freedom...doing what we want. Now that I am older, I really don't care about birthdays or roller coasters and there's little I care to watch on TV. All I think about is being young again. And what I would have done differently if given the chance. Ironically, there is another old saying that goes, "Youth is too precious to waste on young people." You have to think about that for a second or two, but as many look back on their lives, that statement is rings true.

Being young for me was a glorious time. When I was first married, I used to write some poetry. I was in love, idealistic, and happy! Here's a poem I wrote when I was 23 years old:

> **Life is Worth the Living**
> *For life to be worth the living*
> *One must have a God worth serving*
> *Of all the gods to choose from*
> *There can only be One deserving*
> *The Lord Jesus Christ is my choice*
> *He outshines the others by far*
> *His loving compassion continues*
> *To be my guiding star*
> *He sits at the right had of the Father*
> *The Spirit reveals His will*

He prepares a mansion before us
His plan we're destine to fulfill
We love him because He first loved us
Before we were borne, He died
He knows your innermost being
In Him you can confide

Here's a special note to my grandchildren: I often sent your Mother, Rosemary, pictures of you as you were growing up at various ages, reminding her of how short a time she has with you. However, for parents, the days are often long and hard, where worries and problems never seem to end and time seems to drag. Parents often wish for the next phase of life to pass. They dream about you beginning to talk and walk, when you will conquer potty training, when you lose your baby teeth, when you graduate, when you will get married, and, of course, when you give them grandchildren! But practically speaking, time is a funny thing, where "the days are long, but the years are short." Looking back on my life, I understand that truth completely.

Life is but a vapor. It will end in a flash, sooner for some than others; no one knows the length of our days. You must live every day to the fullest. Have a great attitude in the morning, be productive during the day, and thank God for your life at night when you lay your head on the pillow. This path is not easy, but I offer this advice with all my love.

Most people have regrets. I certainly do. And depending on how you face adversity, you will either be satisfied or regretful when you look back on your lives. When I retired from the Air Force in December 2003, I had some thoughts on regrets. I was 51 years old at the time when I delivered these remarks at my retirement ceremony at Hill AFB in Utah:

"Many people say they don't have any regrets at this point. That's not true for me. Beginning with the Academy, I wish I would have studied harder, gotten more involved in flying (glider program), and taken more advantage of the cadet leadership opportunities. I was involved in leadership, but that was confined to athletic teams, social events and Christian groups. In retrospect, I missed some great chances to develop leadership skills in the cadet laboratory.

In my Air Force career, I wish I had worked harder and taken more responsibility as a younger officer. I wish I would have taken a Pentagon assignment that I was offered. In investing, I wish I would have kept with my long-term strategy developed as a 2LT. I wish I wouldn't have washed out of pilot training. I attribute my failure in pilot training to underestimating the degree of difficulty that flying a jet aircraft really was and is. Even though I soloed the T-37 and T-38 jet aircraft, I failed to prepare adequately for flights, failed to thoroughly learn procedures, failed to chair-fly enough, lacked self-discipline in flying operations, and was impacted by some personal circumstances. Having said that, I had a great life growing up as a Weapon Systems Officer in the F-111, and today I fly better than some pilots, so it wasn't all a loss – just a different path. One regret I don't have is spending more time with my wife and children; partially by design and partially by the choice of assignments, I was fortunate enough to be with my wife and children almost all of our 30-year career."

Everything that you do in life is significant. Someday you will be face-to-face with God and there will be an accounting. Apply yourself and strive to constantly and consistently please God. He is the One that ultimately matters. Remember it's His rules and his creation, not ours.

You will reap what you sow

One of the lowest and most trying times in my life came when I was in the Air Force. My Wing Commander had it out for me, and he wasn't letting up. No matter what it took, he didn't want me to fly again or get promoted. Worse than that, he wanted me out of the Air Force and having me end up in prison would have been icing on the cake for him.

To make a very long story short, (the details are in my book "Renegade Colonel") the Wing Commander succeeded in forcing me to resign from the Air Force, but he didn't have the last word. It took nearly four years of my life to bounce back. I was re-instated in the Air Force, and back promoted to Major, made Lt Colonel, and finally retired a Colonel, same rank as that Wing Commander when he retired. I was one of the very few in the Air Force that beat City Hall and came back....Only by the grace of God!

During this ordeal, I had a very wise Black non-commissioned officer (NCO) tell me, "Don't worry Mr. Bill, what goes around comes around". Most people on the base saw the situation for what it was, but this Wing Commander had me by the short hairs and he was going to yank! But the wise NCO turned out to be right in the end.

Your decisions determine your destiny. God and my friends had my back. I stayed the course, knowing you reap what you sow.

There are circumstances in life that you can't control. Stay the course. Things change. Make the mature judgement, which is a tough thing to do when you are young and under pressure. Don't choose instant gratification. View life in the long term. Robert Lewis Stevenson once said, "Don't judge each day by the harvest you reap, but by the seeds that you plant." He was just saying, you reap what you sow.

God didn't give us Ten Suggestions. He gave us Ten Commandments. If you want to have a better life, you must consider them mandatory. They will shield you from harm and give you a happier life. Unfortunately, many of us, myself included, have to let experience teach us. And experience is a very good teacher in most cases. If you learn from your experience, then you are a very good student. Some people are poor students of life's lessons. Observe, and don't be one of those people. I have a little saying I used with Luke, my Grandson: "Some people learn the easy way, and some people learn the hard way. But, in the end, we all learn." A little hint here: Drugs and alcohol are not your friends. I hope you don't have to learn this the hard way.

The Bible says, *"Let your light so shine before men that they will see your good works and glorify your Father who is in heaven."* For the long term, what you invest in turns out to be a good or bad investment. Make good investments in your body, mind and spirit. You will reap what you sow in this life and the next.

Follow God's Commands

Simply put, do what God says! No one likes to get a whipping, but obedience requires discipline. Obedience and faithfulness to God's will brings happiness, joy, and blessings! Why is it so hard to obey? Because it's against our human nature. We must be disciplined to do what is right. As we see in *Psalms 19:8*, "The commandments of the LORD are right, bringing joy to the heart. The commands of the LORD are clear, giving insight for living."

Do you want to have a joyful, happy heart? Do you want to have insight for living? Of course you do! Then learn the commandments and obey them! Ask God for strength to choose the narrow way. The easy way leads to death and destruction. The hard way leads to life and happiness. God wants us to have an abundant life. He wants to give us a cup overflowing with gladness! He wants us to experience all the best in life. Although the best in life is different things to different people, God knows what is best for you! He wants to bless you! He wants to give you hope!

In the Book of Jerimiah, 29:11, the Lord is talking to the people of Israel and says to them, and to us as well, "I know the plans I have for you," says the LORD. "They are plans for good and not for disaster, to give you a future and a hope."

Faith in God (Jesus Christ) is your foundation. Build your life on a firm foundation. Know what you believe and why you believe it. You will be tested in your faith, but God will be there with you. He loves you and believes in you more than you can even imagine!

Honor Your Mother & Your Father

Honor your father and mother
Ephesians 6:2

When dealing with computers, it's garbage in, garbage out! The same is true of our lives and our minds. If you want to have excellent output, you must have excellent input.

That's why it's important to read the right books, listen to uplifting music, have the right friends, watch the right kind of TV, expose yourself to the right social media, and get the right education where critical thinking is taught. Believe it or not, when you are in the developmental stage and you're exposed to the wrong things, it can have a devastating effect on your character and the rest of your life. I've seen a series of messages on how an iPhone text can push a young person to commit suicide. How can that happen? It's a complicated process, but the bottom line is emotions ruled the day; a very bad input resulted in a very bad output.

On the other hand, interview successful people. Without fail you will find no matter what their lot in life was to begin with, whether it was poor parents, no money, bad neighborhood, lousy schools, etc., somehow or another, they found a way to claw themselves out of those circumstances and sow good input into their lives. Avoid drugs and alcohol! They will do you no good, hamper your success, and if abused will leave you homeless in bad health waiting to die.

Other people were given a golden spoon from birth, yet they chose not to eat. You are responsible for the input you allow to influence your character. Not all the time, but most of the time, you can control the input, which after germination, becomes the output. Guard your heart and mind as you grow up. It is so important to choose the right friends and listen to your parents when you are growing up. And, once again, don't forget to find and hang on to great friends and great mentors!

Don't ever forget that the first and best mentors, if you're lucky, are your parents. In fact, the full Bible quote I started this section with comes from the Book of Ephesians, 6:1-3: is *"Children, obey your parents. Children, obey your parents because you belong to the Lord, for this is the right thing to do. Honor your father and mother. This is the first commandment with a promise: If you honor your father and mother, "...things will go well for you, and you will have a long life on the earth."*

Life Lesson #2 — Family and Friends

Get a Mentor

Find a mentor and don't let go! Choose those people who you love and admire and spend life with them! Hopefully they will love you as much as you love them, but find someone who has life figured out and do what they do. Think like they think. Become close to them and never let go. They can help form your person and character when you are unable to do it yourself. Take their advice. Make them your heroes. Mimic what they do and say. Get close to them and their families. They will bless you for life. They will teach you. They will guide you. They will love you and support you unconditionally. They will make you a better person. There's wisdom in many counselors. These people are like water to a parched land. They were life for me.

Because my Mom and Dad divorced when I was a little boy, my father was mostly absent from my life. Hopefully your prime mentor will be your father. That is God's design, but we have some selfish, flawed men out there who father children and then leave them to fend for themselves.

Hopefully your father is a kind and loving man. It's a fact that children develop their initial concept of God from their earthly fathers. Sometimes that's a good thing, sometimes not. It may take a lifetime to overcome a flawed father, but without professional help, some men and women never do.

God gave me three mentors when I was in high school and in my early Air Force Academy years to fill in for my missing Dad. These men profoundly affected my life, my beliefs, my worldview, who I married, and how I raised my children.

Sometimes mentors reach the level of hero. My three hero mentors were: James Jeffrey, past Executive President of the Fellowship of Christian Athletes, who died of pancreatic cancer years ago; General (USAF, Retired) Orwyn Sampson, Department Head of Biology at the US Air Force Academy; and General (USAF, Retired) Dick Abel, who commissioned me and officiated at my Air Force retirement in December 2003. (I'm sorry to report that he passed away this year before this book was published) It's impossible to underestimate their influence in my life, and my gratitude for the time and effort they put into my development as a person.

James Jeffrey once said, "If you are to see life to a worthy conclusion, you must remember those that love you are watching you, and they are expecting the greatest from you. And you must not disappoint that love." You could live a lifetime on those words, yet he had so much other wisdom to offer me while he was alive. He was always such an encourager.

After one particularly challenging time in our lives he said, "Bill, there will be a time in the not-too-distant future when all your options will be good ones," And he followed that up with, "Bill, I know two great people in all the world – and you're both of them!" Wow, what a guy! Gen Abel and Gen Sampson have been equally supportive and encouraging to me and my family. I could never repay them for their investments in me and subsequently to the Murray family.

I would be remiss if I didn't mention another fabulous fourth mentor: Colonel (USAF, Retired) Ray Leach. He is 85 today. I have known Ray since he was an F-111 Squadron Commander at Cannon AFB some 43 years ago. I was overjoyed when I found out God put us together again in our retirement years in Dallas, Texas, where since 2004, he has been an especially close friend and mentor. He refers to me fondly as "the son he never had" (he has three beautiful daughters) and I refer to him as "the best!" We play golf, commiserate about the state of our country, talk about our wives and children, and generally solve most of the world's problems on the golf course or phone, (I call him every night) or when we're together in person.

Ray is true blue. He's a man of uncompromising integrity, a lover of dogs, solid character, old school in every way, and would do anything I asked of him, if he had the capacity. We have had many great conversations, meals and golf rounds over the years, and I am a better man for his influence and perspective in my life.

Ray has given me sage wisdom concerning my eight years of employment with Lockheed Martin, where I was a senior systems engineer on the F-22 and the F-35 stealth 5th generation fighters. I could easily write another book about Lockheed Martin and the Defense Industrial Complex, but I would be thrown into prison if I did. Ray has also weighed in many times with perspective, encouragement and guidance concerning my ten years of employment with American Airlines as a pilot instructor. He's always in my corner and I know it, and I feel it.

I would be remiss again, if I didn't mention another mentor in my later life............A fifth mentor! His name is Admiral Willy Moore. He reminds me a lot of James Jeffrey. He's a charismatic leader who knows how to command an audience with unbelievable stories that touch people's hearts. I first met him at Lockheed Martin when I was working on the F-35 Program and he was the Vice President of Sustainment.

I was a nobody, but he always had time for me. I had no influence, but he always wanted to hear my perspective. I didn't matter to the company, but he encouraged me like I was a Director of Programs. We still get together even though he is retired and I'm working for American Airlines. I just like to be around him. He's one of those people I don't want to let go of! I value his time and his friendship. He is a man among men, a true blue....just like Ray!

Finally, there's Dr. James Dobson, a sixth mentor! Even though I don't know him personally, I've read most of his books, newsletters, and subscribe to just about everything he teaches. I feel like I've known him all my life! He has influenced my thinking in many positive ways. My children joke that they believe they were raised by Dr. Dobson and his book, "Dare to Discipline". He's a giant man of faith. He's a man with an unrelenting desire to please God and use his talents to solve problems and help families.

Some people never have a James Jeffrey, a General Abel, a General Sampson, a Colonel Leach, an Admiral Moore, or a Dr. James Dobson in their lives, but I have been fortunate to have six, and that doesn't even account for so many others, professional or close friends, who have mentored me and made me who I am today.

Get yourself a mentor or two or more! They are worth their weight in gold. And that goes for my daughters and Granddaughter also. In spite of your Mother's great influence, find yourself a woman who you admire. You know Mom chose Mrs Johnson, wife of the Head Chaplin at the Air Force Academy when I was there, as the person she most wanted to be like when she became a Grandmother. No one is more loving than Mrs Johnson or put her family first at every turn than she did! And I wanted your Mother to be like Mrs Johnson in every way she could be!

Great Teachers

Tell me and I forget. Teach me and I remember. Involve me and I learn.

Benjamin Franklin

Great mentors are great teachers. Great teachers always provide a true perspective by presenting the big picture first. Then they drill down and demonstrate how the current topic fits into the big picture. Great teachers are passionate about their subject. They are enthusiastic! They are well prepared. They care about their students and will find whatever vehicle it takes to help them learn. If you think about it, some of the most influential people in your early life were your teachers.

I always ask my student pilots, "How do pilots learn?" After some perplexing looks, I say, "Repetition, repetition, repetition!" Yes, you learn by making errors; you learn by study and presentations; and you learn from experience. But, there are many subjects you will never learn on just the first pass-through. It takes multiple reviews. Furthermore, most people are tactile learners. They have to touch it, feel it, and see how it moves before they really learn about a system.

Teaching is a gift. You only have to be in a classroom a short time before you know whether your teacher is excellent, average, or poor. You can tell whether the teacher is enjoying the experience and has a passion for their subject, or whether they are just going through the motions. We owe so much to good teachers. Think back to high school. Ingrained in your memories are your best teachers. They had an influence on your character and your life. They are to be honored.

Be careful who you trust

Trust, but verify

Ronald Reagan

Concerning your personal affairs, be careful who you trust! This is especially true concerning financial planners, healthcare workers (yes, including doctors and surgeons), attorneys, real estate agents, counselors, and even your pastors. Carefully oversee their work. You are ultimately responsible for your decisions, so don't be lazy. Read the documents and pay attention to the details. Their primary concern is what is going on in their life, not yours! This is especially true if you are the head of a household.

I have a great friend from Tennessee that I met in the Air Force. His name is Kenny Caldwell. He was enlisted, but on his own initiative, he got his Bachelor's and his Master's degrees while in the Air Force, although it was not required for an enlisted person. He married a beautiful young gal. Her name is Tina. They did things the right way. The had aspirations and visions for their future and they made wise decisions. We met them when they were trying to be better partners in their marriage by attending our Bible Study on marriage.

They had a strong marriage. They were just trying to make it stronger through learning solid life-time principles and find older mentors who demonstrated those principles in their lifelong union. Judy and I have always been very transparent about our highs and lows in our marriage and Kenny and Tina took advantage of those lessons. I wish every young couple were like Kenny and Tina.

It's not a surprise that when Kenny left the Air Force early to return to his beloved Tennessee, that his life continued to flourish. They had three beautiful children and he became the CFO of a medical company. This did not happen by accident. He is a hard, hard worker, a great husband and a great father. He has been successful in every area of his life, because he had the right values and he worked hard.

We have talked many times through the years. He has a great sense of humor and we love to compare notes on subjects like where we are financially, where we are with our families, and generally other important subjects that impact our lives. I remember a story he told me about doctors and their finances. He had a job once where he managed the financial accounts of a number of doctors. He said whenever he was in a meeting and the doctors were discussing care vs profit, there was always a doctor that felt like he was obligated to say, "This has nothing to do with profit.". To that, Kenny told me revealing their true motivation, "You can bet your bottom dollar on one thing: What is about to follow has everything to do with profit!"

Planning in life is important, and financial planning is equally important. Find someone that you trust to help you plan financially and in life in general. Again, that's why mentors are important. You can bounce your ideas against them and get many great points of view in all the aspects of life, but especially your personal affairs, where you will inevitably find challenges.

Choose your Mate Wisely!

This life lesson is so, so important. Making a mistake here has the potential to wreck your entire life. Some people recover from marrying the wrong person, and some people never do. People who marry the right person enjoy a lifetime of blessings. Yes, they have trials.

Everyone does. But they face their trials as a team and come up with good, logical solutions to get them out of the ditch.

The Apostle Paul, in the Second Book Of Corinthians, 4:17-18, assures us we will have trials in our lives: "For our present troubles are small and won't last very long. Yet they produce for us a glory that vastly outweighs them and will last forever! So, we don't look at the troubles we can see now; rather, we fix our gaze on things that cannot be seen. For the things we see now will soon be gone, but the things we cannot see will last forever."

I dated many girls prior to finding the love of my life, Judy. I fall in love easily, but that's just because I love people, and I am influenced by feelings to a great degree. I'm not necessarily advocating dating a lot of people before you marry, but I do advocate getting to know lots of people of the opposite sex. It's the only way you can discern which characteristics you're looking for in your life partner, before you enter into a life-long covenant.

And one more vital point. You not only marry the girl; you marry her family. Write this down and underline it. It is ground in truth. You may think you're going to only be with her in a cottage out in the woods, but that is far from the truth. Both families will be a huge part of your marriage!

I am just as in love with my wife, Judy, today as I was the day I met her 48 years ago. We are as different as night and day, but we know each other well, and most of the time we work together well. Here's my story from my first book, "Renegade Colonel", about meeting her. I want you to notice how I was trying to reason (use my brain), but my feelings (dictated by my heart) were fighting for control.

Judy

In March of my Junior year, I was about to go to a dance that would change my life. It was a providential meeting to say the very least. The Lord was in this meeting. Ordinarily, I didn't go to cadet dances. I didn't like them. Cadets fondly called them "Cattle Calls". The story was always the same – there were about 100 girls bussed in from all over the Colorado area. Of the 100 girls there were about 2 of them that were beautiful.

The cadets would start drinking and soon most of the staggering cadets would be hovering around the two beautiful girls doing anything to gain their attention – acting silly and saying stupid stuff. The other 98 girls stood quietly on the sidelines making small talk among themselves. I felt sorry for the 98 girls and didn't like the drunken cadets slobbering over the 2 beautiful girls, so that's why I never went to cadet dances – I didn't like the scene.

However, it was a Friday night and we didn't have anything to do. Our squadron had a dance at Temple Buell College, or Colorado Women's College as it's known today. Six of us who went to Bible Study and hung out with each other decided to drive to Denver to check things out just for a change. Mac, Stick, Jerry (who borrowed the car), Dave, Hud, Gary and I left for Denver on an Off Duty Privilege (ODP) – this was a pass to leave *the Academy grounds, but you had to return by 1:00 AM that same evening to sign in. Sometimes it's just nice to get away from the Academy, so this was the perfect opportunity to blow off some steam and escape for a few hours.*

When we got to Temple Buele we gathered in the foyer right by the dance area trying to figure out where to go next. Right away we saw four gorgeous girls walking down the stairs and coming around the corner. They walk over to us and I said under my breath, "We've already doubled the odds from our normal outings" – meaning that there were four beautiful women instead of the normal two. No kidding these gals were strikingly beautiful and they all seemed to have a common look.

They walked up and we starting talking with them right away. They asked where we were from. I said, "You can't guess" meaning that anyone at that time who had short hair was either from the Academy or Ft Carson (the Army base) and I hoped they didn't think we were Army soldiers. They said, "No, we have no idea where you're from."

Reluctantly we admitted, "We go to the Academy". Immediately they respond, "Where's that?" I said, "Let's get out of here." Even though these girls seemed nice, I didn't like people who were fake. Everyone in Colorado knew where the Academy was. I thought they were playing us up. I wasn't falling for it. I started to walk away. Then they said, "No, no, we don't know where the Academy is. We're not from here. We're from Texas!"

I knew there was something funny about their accents. "Texas. No kidding – what are you doing up here?" They went on to say they were sisters traveling with their Mom and Dad in a motor home and visiting their cousin Susan who went to Temple Buele. They also said later that Susan told them not to go to the dance because there was "only one thing those cadets were after". They just laughed and said we couldn't be much worse than the guys in Texas.

These girls kind of intimidated me. When they talked they used their hands to talk. They couldn't say anything without touching your arm or shoulder. I wasn't used to that. Why couldn't they just say it without touching us? I stood around the corner of the door while we talked. These girls were fun but they were so forward. I was a little off balance.

I liked Judy right away. She was the big sister. She had a red flowered blouse on and she was the most beautiful girl I had ever seen in my life – and I had seen lots of beautiful girls. She had a natural beauty with a perfect complexion. She was tall and carried herself confidently.

Her hair was teased up and it enhanced the beauty of her look. When she smiled her whole face lit up. She had the nicest, most sincere smile. I could see a kindness in her eyes. She wore a turquoise eye shadow that made her eyes gleam. The more she talked, the more I was drawn to her. She was radiant. All four girls were beautiful but I liked Judy. It was love at first sight. I was smitten from the first time I saw her.

After we had done some small talk, the guys asked if they would like to go out to eat – we told them we just came up to the dance on a whim and we didn't really care about going to the dance. They said they were famished and that sounded like a wonderful idea. Immediately the guys began to pair off with the LaQuey sisters. Susan had a date with her boyfriend, so she wasn't part of the equation.

When the pairing was complete Mac matched up with Judy, Hud was matched with Kathy, Jerry with Teresa, and Stick with Christy. Gary and I were on the outside looking in. When the girls got wind of the match-up, they encouraged us all to go out as a group. They didn't want dates. That was a nice sentiment but we were going to pay for their dinners so we saw matching up as a necessity. And I was never one to fight for girls. Besides, I wasn't supposed to be dating anyway. So Gary and I stayed behind and talked a little and phoned some friends we had in Denver. The guys took them out to the Spaghetti Warehouse in Denver and were gone for a couple of hours.

While they were gone, all I could think about was how I was going to connect up again with Judy. They had told us they were only in town for one night – a temporary stop to see Susan on their way to see California and Susan's family over Spring Break. Providence – a moment in time. Even though she was outwardly beautiful, I could see an inner beauty to her that attracted me even more. I like her and the way she carried herself. The only sticking point for me would be if she was a Christian or not. If she wasn't, that would be a show stopper. I wasn't into evangelistic dating – where you went out with a girl just to try to bring her to the Lord.

When they got back, everyone had had a wonderful time – they were laughing and joking as they walked up to the college. And I'll never forget the moment. It was like a scene out of "Love Story" – even though it was only March, the biggest snowflakes started to fall out of the moonlit sky. Of course the girls from Texas really ate that up. They hadn't seen a lot of snow in their lives – and never in March.

It was romantic. It was a moment in time. I was relishing the moment. I went right up to Judy and said I was sorry I didn't come to dinner. She said something like she really wished I could have come with them – that they had so much fun eating out together. I got her address and phone number at Southwest Texas State University where she was a Junior just like me and I promised to write or call her sometime in the future. She said that would be great and looked forward to talking with me again.

I love this story. Everyone has a love story, but ours is the best! Notice my feelings……I was a goner, but I also was looking for a woman of a certain character, one who could be the Mother of my children. A good value for anyone looking for a wife.

***I Must Have Been in Love ***

Driving home, I was flying high. I knew I had to get in touch with Judy somehow. I was a little giddy when I went to bed that night. She was a beautiful gal – she still is, nearly 33 ½ years later. She still has that inner and outer beauty and I am so glad the Lord brought us together that night. It was a night to remember and the details are still fixed in my mind's eye.

Even though I knew I wanted to get together with Judy, somehow in the back of my mind I knew it was a dream. I was in the middle of a tough academic semester, in the middle of lacrosse season, and in the middle of a bunch of spiritual stuff. Plus, she was in Texas and I was in Colorado. I did ask her if she was dating anyone steadily and she said no which stunned me. All her sisters were just like her. I could tell they were a close family and I liked that about all of them. I could tell they had an allegiance with each other.

I waited until I knew they were back from California and in school before I made the call. My heart was pounding and my palms were sweaty. I was hoping she would remember me. A girl answered the phone, "Judy?" "No this is Teresa. I'm in Dallas and this is our home number. Judy is in college down in San Marcos. Do you have that number?" "No" I said. "Could you give it to me?" I didn't want to make two long distance calls to reach her (remember calling long distance at that time was expensive), but I thought this might be an investment.

Finally, I got her on the phone. I explained that the guys forced me into the phone booth and wouldn't let me out until I called her. She just laughed and said "Sure". I can't remember how long we talked or what we talked about but I remember she sounded as nice and wonderful as I had remembered. I told her I would call again soon. I could tell that we would get along.

And that's how it started. I called pretty regularly and discovered she wasn't attached to anyone – that she was the President of her sorority (Alpha Xi Delta) and that she was a Catholic. I asked her about that and determined she had a sincere faith in God and that it was important to her. I talked about my relationship with God and how important that was to me and that didn't seem to scare her off. In fact, I think she kind of liked the fact that spiritual things were a priority in my life. We were both extremely busy at our schools with friends and activities but we continued to correspond.

In this next section, notice how Judy relied on the advice of her Father, and notice how I wanted her to get to know my mentors Pastor and Mrs Johnson for a second opinion.

*** Invitation to the Ring Dance ***

Pretty soon the idea popped into my mind to invite her to the Spring Ring Dance. I could fly her up and she could stay with Chaplain and Mrs. Johnson. What a great idea – even though we weren't serious we could do it for fun and just have a week of parties, parades and festivities prior to my summer training before my senior year. The more I thought about it the more I liked the idea. Stick thought it was a good idea also. He liked Judy too. Most of my friends had steady girls they were inviting to the Ring Dance.

When I talked to Judy about the idea of flying up and staying with the Johnson's I'll never forget her response. "Well, that sounds like a lot of fun, but I'll have to check with my parents and get back with you." Now that really impressed me. Even though we were 21 years old, I was still wondering how she would respond. I knew plenty of girls who would jump at the chance to come up to the Academy and be glad to stay in a motel with some guy, so I was very curious how she would respond to my offer.

She responded perfectly, wanting to talk it over with her parents first. And she didn't balk at the idea of staying with the Chaplain. That impressed me too. I was beginning to really like this girl.

She got back with me and said that her parents thought it would be all right for her to travel up for the week. So, everything was set. It was April now. The dance was in June. I went to the travel agency at the Academy, purchased the airplane tickets, insured them, and sent them to her in the mail. She got them in a few days and we began to plan the week. I told her that most guys invited someone that they had been dating for some time and a lot of guys got engaged that week, so I hoped she didn't mind going with me just for fun. She said she was looking forward to it. I wanted to show her the beauty of Colorado and introduce her to all my Christian friends, classmates, and Uncle Bill and Auntie Jen.

*** Forget You Met Me ***

I had just sent Judy the airline tickets for the Ring Dance, so I had to tell her what happened. The Ring Dance was definitely off, so I got in the phone both again and decided to tell her the details. She was so excited to hear from me. I remember my first words to her. "You're not going to believe what happened but it's probably best if you forget you ever met me. I'm in big, big trouble." And I remember her response, "It couldn't be that bad. What happened?" I assured her it was that bad and worse. I told her at that point I probably wouldn't graduate, and if I avoided prison time, I would be lucky. We had burned down a guy's room and he was lucky to get out alive – that was the only bright spot in this whole deal – no one got hurt. I told her it would be best if she just forgot we ever met.

The next couple of weeks were tense. Both Stick and I shined our shoes, cleaned up our room and got real short haircuts – and we laid low. This thing could go anywhere. We knew no matter what was decided, we were toast. That was the bottom line – toast, burnt toast!

I'm not sure how it was decided or who decided it, but they dropped the idea of civil charges and dismissal from the Academy. They opted instead for a Cadet Disciplinary Board (CDB). The CDB was a mere formality. They gave us the maximum they could give – loss of our cars for our senior year, six months of restrictions and 120 tours – 120 hours of marching in step to the beat of a drum on the Terrazzo in our Class A Uniform on our free time. They threw the book at us, but I felt lucky just to be able to have the chance to graduate. Just as in waiting for a decision about what would happen to us, there would be more waiting to see when the punishments would take effect. Our case had yet to go through many review levels prior to us serving our punishments. That meant that for the time being we didn't have to be restricted to campus or march any tours until the punishments were formally handed down.

They say timing is everything. Things were coming to a crunch because we only had about three weeks to go until the Ring Dance. Stick was dating a beautiful girl from Missouri named Jayne Lineberry who would eventually be his wife. Stick had invited Jayne out for the Ring Dance like I did Judy. When Stick and I talked about it, we decided to call the girls and tell them just to forget about coming. We were sure our punishment was just around the corner, or the administration would levy our punishment right before June Week (when the Ring Dance and festivities at the end of the year started) just to turn the screws a little bit.

There were some officers that thought our cadet punishment was far too weak for the crime. In any event, I was sick to think I wasn't going to have Judy up here for this *celebratory occasion. I was really looking forward to seeing her again.*

When I talked with her again on the phone, she continued to make light of the situation. "Oh, it can't be that bad" she said kind of laughing. "I'm sure we can work something out." I admired her optimism, but I knew the facts and the intent of the administration. They wanted to put the last nail in our coffins and they weren't kidding around.

Then Judy said, "Why don't I just drive up to Colorado Springs? That way when your punishments come down, I could just drive home." My optimism perked a little. I really did want to see her, but I didn't want her to have to drive all the way up to Colorado for just one day. I suggested she talk to her Dad about that idea. He was an over-the-road truck driver – he would be able to tell her how long a drive it would be and approve the trip. I told her I thought it was about eight hours. This is still a joke in our family today because the drive was actually 13-14 hours even at 65 mph, but for some reason she never asked her Dad about how long the drive would be. He was more concerned about whether her 1969 Firebird would safely make the trip.

*** Judy Drives to USAFA ***

I talked with Stick about the idea. Stick thought It piqued his interest also for Jayne could do the same thing, and in the end, both gals made the drive when the punishments had not come down by the Friday prior to June Week starting. I couldn't believe we made it that far, but I wanted to see Judy so badly at that point that even one day would be worth it. She drove up on a Friday. She left with a credit card and $5 cash in her purse. She was as in love as I was – no one was thinking clearly. She called me from Harmon Hall when she arrived late in the day.

She looked great – better than I had remembered. Even though we hadn't seen each other since March, we had talked about lots of things on the phone and exchanged a few letters. I felt like I knew her fairly well but I wanted to get to know her better. One thing was really bothering me though – it concerned drinking. Right around Judy's birthday (May 6th), three days after mine, she sent me a picture of her holding a board game. The game was called "The Pink Elephant".

That didn't mean anything to me, but when I showed her picture to some of the guys in the squadron there were some "ooze and awes" – they told me that The Pink Elephant was a drinking game where you made your way around the board trying to win the game without passing out. Oh great – that's all I needed. The guys were really giving me the business because they knew I didn't drink. They said, "You've really got a wild woman on your hands now, Murray!"

At this point in my life, I didn't drink at all. I never drank beer and I didn't particularly like other kinds of liquor, and my main concern was my Christian witness and my example to my younger brothers who were both still in high school. If they got into trouble drinking, I didn't want it to be because of my bad example. I gave some thought and prayer as to how I was going to handle this issue. I wouldn't bring it up right when I saw her, but within the first couple of days I had decided I was going to have to tell her how I felt about drinking – and if she was a big drinker that would be a problem.

I didn't know what to do when I first saw, her so I suggested we take a little drive around the Academy grounds. She just laughed and said that was the last thing she wanted to do – she had just spent 14 hours in the car driving to get there. All she wanted to do was get out of that car! So, then I suggested we take a short walk across the street and look at a picturesque lake right across from Harmon Hall. She thought that would be a much better idea.

It was just great to be with her. I couldn't believe how long it had taken her to drive up. I never believed it would have been that long of a drive. We walked along slowly – the terrain along the edge of the water was rocky and jagged. Judy was having trouble keeping her balance. I knew I should take her hand and help her along, but I didn't want to seem to forward by holding hands with her the first day, so I let her stumble along until I couldn't stand it. Finally, I said, "Here I'll help you" and I took hold of her arm just above the wrist.

"Boy this is stupid" I thought to myself. So, I slid my hand down into hers. We were holding hands. It felt great, but I was a little embarrassed and thought things were moving a little fast. We talked about her trip, her family and our plans for the week, always being cautious to caveat things by saying my punishments could come down at any time and she would have to go home and I would have to start marching tours.

Stick got together with Jayne and was having a wonderful time also but both of us operated under the cloud of when the punishments would come raining down. We were trying not to think about it. All we wanted to do was to enjoy the moment. And it was a great time – even though we wouldn't be getting our cars, we were completing our Junior year, getting our rings and we were starting our senior year – only twelve more months and we would be free – 2nd Lieutenants and off to pilot training. It was the next carrot to keep us going.

I took Judy over to meet Chaplain and Mrs. Johnson. Like all people that meet her even today – they were taken up with her. She endeared herself to them by just being herself. I liked her and I could tell they liked her also. She was fun and fun loving. She smiled and her smile lit up the room. I didn't want to leave her that night but I had to get back to the dorm, and she needed some time to unwind, get settled in, and get ready for a full day I had planned for the next day.

Notice here that I took the one I loved the most to meet my family in the area, whom I loved the most. Also notice that certain values were important to me that I had learned from my mentors. Notice also I hadn't lost my sense of humor or joking around, but my judgement might have been clouded when I decided to drive Judy back to Dallas when I was not on leave from the Air Force Academy. Or maybe it was just as my sister Cindy has said for a long time, "When the Murray Boys were born, someone forgot to include the judgment gene"!

*** Driving to Denver***

The first place I wanted to take her was to Denver to meet Uncle Bill and Auntie Jen. I just knew they would love her and I wanted her to meet them and see their home. I still had the issue of discussing the drinking which was making me a little nervous. The more I was around her, the more I liked her and the more I liked her, the harder it was going to be to be without her if some of the major parameters didn't match up.

We took her car to Denver and she let me drive. We did small talk for a short time. I knew it was time. I blurted out, "You know I'm not really a drinker" and I waited uneasily for her response which I'll never forget. "Gosh that's not a big deal – neither am I!" I didn't believe her. I asked about the Pink Elephant game and she just laughed. She said that was given to her as a joke. Then I told her about all the ribbing I had been getting being a Christian and being the Vice President of FCA. She thought that was strange. We gradually moved to talking about her faith, family and friends. I liked everything I heard. I could tell family was very important to her. The

60-minute drive seemed to take 10 minutes. I couldn't believe how fast we got there.

Auntie Jen and Uncle Bill were ready as usual. They gave her a warm welcome and started bringing out the snacks. I ate them but Judy didn't eat much. We visited for a long time and I listened very carefully to her responses. She was very much at ease around my family – I liked that. I can't remember what we did the rest of the day or that night, but I was smitten by the love bug. I was falling fast and everything was matching up. I had dated enough girls to know that Judy was in a category of her own. Heck, I had even dated Miss Colorado and she couldn't hold a candle to Judy!

Could this be the reason that the Lord had urged me not to date for six months? Could this be the girl that the Lord had planned for me to spend the rest of my life with? I didn't even want to tempt myself to entertain the thought. I just wanted to enjoy my time with her. I wanted to get to know her and I wanted her to get to know me and share with her what was important in my life. She was having a good time and so was I. The next day we went to Protestant services at the Academy Chapel. Chaplain Johnson gave a wonderful sermon as usual. The Academy Chapel is an impressive structure and makes you feel closer to the Lord just being in there.

*** The Ring ***

Judy and I had an absolutely wonderful time together that week. We did all kinds of stuff together. I introduced her to my friends, showed her all around the Academy, and attended all the functions. Poor Stick marched his tours and came to the Ring Dance alone. I felt awful, but at that time didn't know why his punishments came down and mine didn't. Stick and I got our picture taken together under the Class Ring since Jayne couldn't be there. I still have the picture. It was fitting we were such *good friends and nearly left the Academy together. Stick married Jayne and is a Captain for Northwest Airlines today. He did all right. Stick and I both got white stones in our rings. Most guys got blue ones but we wanted to do something different.*

I would come back to my room each night talking about Judy. The guys knew I was falling head over heels for her. I couldn't think of anything I didn't like about her. I asked them if I should give her an engagement ring at the end of the week – they all laughed about that. Then I had an idea. This would be a great prank and show me whether Judy had a sense of humor. I decided to buy a fake diamond ring and give it to Judy in front of my buddies on the last night. I ran the idea past Judy and she thought it would be funny.

We made our little plan and I asked all the guys to come out to the quadrangle for something really special. About 8-10 guys came out for the greatly anticipated excitement. They surrounded Judy and me, and I pulled out the ring – a solitaire diamond about a carat in size. I flashed the ring and said "Judy, I love you. Will you marry me?" and I put the ring on her finger. I heard some of the guys say under their breath, "He really did it." At first she smiled and put the ring on her finger but then she did something to show me her acting skills and innovative abilities – it was hilarious and added credibility to our little prank.

All of the sudden she gets this stricken look on her face and says, "No, no I can't do this. It's too soon!" And she takes off the ring and throws it into the rocks on the ground. I immediately dive to the ground groping for the ring in the rocks. I hear someone say, "Oh boy – I'm out of here!" and that's when we tell them it was all an act. We laughed and laughed. How funny – I only wished at this point our engagement was real.

*** Driving to Dallas ***

When the time came for Judy to drive back to Dallas I couldn't bear the thought of her driving those 14 hours back alone. The problem was I couldn't leave the Academy. This is the part in the story where love trumps judgment. I simply told her that I was going to drive her home, meet her family and fly back the next day. No one would ever miss me – I thought.

We had a great time driving through the Colorado mountains down through Raton Pass across New Mexico (where we would be stationed later in our married life) and finally the short eight hours through Texas – maybe that's the eight hours I was thinking about earlier. The weather was very hot in Texas in June and there wasn't a cloud in the sky. Judy's car had terrible air conditioning, so I asked her if she minded me taking off my shirt. She hesitated but knew how hot it was.

As we got about a block from her house I said we need to pull over so I can put my shirt on – no way was I going to meet her family with my shirt off. We pulled to the side of the road and no sooner than I get my shirt started over my head than Mrs. LaQuey pulls up behind us in her Texas-sized Cadillac – whoops! "What are you all doing?" "Ma'am, I can explain everything" I said pulling that shirt down as fast as I could. Judy just laughed knowing her Mom was just kidding, but I was pulling that shirt on as fast as it would go. How did this happen?

We exchanged quick howdies and headed for the house. At the time, I thought Mr. LaQuey was the one I had to fear but little did I know Mrs. LaQuey was the one really looking me over. Arriving at her home on Ballymote Drive

I thought, "What have I gotten myself into?" Judy really hadn't said anything about her financial status but after seeing the Cadillac and this big lovely home with a swim pool and large bathhouse out back (with the same front as the regular house) I knew they were rich – which made me more uncomfortable. (I can picture the rest of the family chuckling right now).

We went into the house and I met everyone that was there – Teresa, Kathy, Christy, Bobby and her Father. Mr. LaQuey was a big man, a little smaller than me, who looked you straight in the eye and had a welcoming smile. I soon learned he knew lots about the Air Force Academy. He and I talked for a while and I liked him right away. I liked Mrs. LaQuey also. She was beautiful and full of energy. All the family was friendly and seemed happy that I took the time and effort to drive Judy back to Texas. We told them all about our week and all the festivities we did together. The girls just giggled.

Mrs. LaQuey made a big dinner for everyone of chicken fried steak, mashed potatoes and gravy. It was great and I was hungry. At that time in my life, I could eat – and not worry about gaining weight. Back then I was big and strong and most of my weight was above my belly – just the opposite of what it is today! We laughed and told stories and I observed things very carefully. Someone told me long ago if you want to see what a girl is going to be like after you marry her, take a long look at her Mother. I liked everything I saw. Mrs. LaQuey was fun loving and friendly. She didn't seem to have a care in the world.

Judy and I stayed up late that night talking about what a good week it had been. I hated to go back, but I had to get back to wrap up the year and go on my official leave which was my first session of the summer. I can't remember what my second training session was but my third was T-41s – my initial flight training. I was really looking forward to that.

I had an early flight back to the Academy the next morning, but Mr. LaQuey wanted me to have biscuits, sausage and gravy before I left. I liked that Southern cooking and hospitality. It was fun being around her family. I promised to come back and see them for one of my weeks of leave in the summer if at all possible. That's providing the Academy would let me leave for my official vacation time, with everything that had happened at the end of the year.

I said good-bye to all the family and Judy drove me to the airport. I told her my plan was to go home to Kansas City for two weeks and then come to Dallas for the last week of my leave if everything worked out. Since I didn't have a car, I would just hitchhike down from KC – it was only eight hours north of Dallas. It was hard leaving. I had determined this was the girl I wanted to marry. She had all the qualities I was looking for in a wife and I could picture her being the Mother of my children. She was perfect for me.

Choose Your Friends Wisely!

Bad company corrupts good character
Corinthians 15:33

My daughters often heard their Mom saying at one time or another, "Choose your friends with care, because like it or not, you become like your friends". Nothing truer could be said about friendships. Social media today is filled with poison relationships. Those relationships begin with simple acquaintances that last too long.

If your friends are not making you a better person, not encouraging you to do the right thing, or not bringing out the best in you, then it's time to make new friends!

That's not an easy thing to do, but until you make the hard choices in life, you will be destined to live a hollow and meaningless life. Why waste your valuable time on people who do not bring out the best in you!

How do you choose friends? When we are young, our parents often make that decision for us. But as we get older, we get a sense of growing independence, and rely less on our parents and more on peer pressure. When this happens, all of the sudden our parents don't know anything, and we come to the erroneous conclusion that you and your peers are the smartest people on earth! And by golly, you're going to make the decision about who you hang with. That experience is natural, but relying on the judgment of peers can be a critical error if you don't use good judgement!

The first step in having good friends is for you to be a good friend yourself. Be friendly, but listen to your conscience. Be a good listener; be an encourager; be a comforter but watch what people do, not what they say! Have empathy, but don't fall into the trap of feeling too sorry for a person who continues to make poor decisions. Choose friends like you would choose a mentor. Select those people that you admire and want to be like, because you will become like your friends! It's natural that you take on the characteristics of your friends. Their "likes" become your "likes", their opinions become your opinions, and sometimes you even dress like them. But if they are not following God's laws or obeying their parents, drop them! You don't need them!

The Apostle Paul reminds us in Ephesians 5:15, "*So be careful how you live. Don't live like fools, but like those who are wise.*" Paul also tells us "*Don't live like a fool.*" Or as Mrs. Abel, General Abel's wife would remind me, "Billy DBD!" (Don't be dumb)

I made some life-long friends on a chance meeting at a mall in Dallas. It was right after I was forced to resign from the Air Force, and I was doing a temporary job in "Marketing". I was getting people at the mall to sign up for the brand-new Discover Card in 1986. To make a long story short, I met this couple who had no interest in talking with me (they were on a special date night at the mall and just enjoying each other when I approached them) but I notice the man had an Academy ring on his finger. I learned he was 1975 graduate of the Naval Academy, and I was a 1975 graduate of the Air Force academy.....God coincidence.

I learned that Robert Hutchins was a Director at E-Systems, the very company I had an interview with the next day. I also learned they had three children and were Christians. So, I detained them longer than they wanted, but immediately I knew I had a bond with the couple, and they invited Judy and me to their church to worship on Sunday!

Again, I'm leaving out lots of details in our friendship, but the next day E-Systems offered me a job, we ended up buying a home in Greenville, Texas, and we ended up going to their church! Imagine that! Over the next three and a half years we got to be very close friends in business, in our families, and in our Christian walk.

The thing that impressed me most about this couple was their yielding to the obedience of the Holy Spirit. As I mentioned, they had three children, but God had been talking to them about how children were a blessing of God, and that they should be limiting God's blessings. In faith they agreed that they were done with birth control and that they would have as many children as The Lord gave them. Talk about faith and obedience. This was a couple to be admired and reverenced. In the end they had seven more children to make ten, and then Nancy got pregnant with twins! Robert joked with me (he's a very quick wit and very smart and very wise) and said, "You know, Bill, they're cheaper by the dozen!"

I have learned many things about walking with God in faith over the last 35+ years, but another story about Robert deserves attention. When he was at the pinnacle of his business career with E-Systems (L-3Comm at this point) and on the verge of being promoted to Vice President and making a lot of money for a long time, God (and Nancy) began talking with him about spending more time at home with his family. Through arduous conversations with God and Nancy and the older children, Robert resigned, bought a small farm, and went home to begin his new career in organic farming, leaving his promising contract career in the dust. This was a man who was serious about listening and obeying God. That was obvious to me, and I couldn't get enough time with him. About 1989, The Lord provided a way for me to have my Air Force career resurrected, and I began to follow God's leading to re-join the Armed Forces as a Major. I hated to leave Robert and Nancy and their dear family and all our new friends in Greenville, but The Lord had new pasture planned for Judy and me also.

I'm happy to say that we have kept in close contact over the years and are still best-of-friends, but I am so happy that God introduced us to one another in that Dallas mall in 1986. Robert is a true-blue friend! Find people like this quality individual and don't let go!

There are givers and takers in this world. Learn how to distinguish between them. Be a giver. Marry a giver. Make friends with those who have a giving spirit. Snuggle up to those who are good listeners and are more interested in you than they are in themselves. Everyone is by nature ego-centric. But find the people who discipline themselves to be interested in the thoughts and feelings of others. Get close to those who make smart, logical, and common-sense decisions over a long time.

That's who you want to emulate and be good friends with your entire life.

Paul Hansen is my best friend in all of life. He learned the principles I wrote about throughout this book from his Dad, and then Paul shared them with me. You won't find a better, truer friend in all the world. Paul and I are as different as night and day. We got acquainted at basic training at Lackland AFB, Texas, in the summer of 1970. That was 52 years ago. Just to show how life can be full of surprises, and how friendships and life-long relationships can present themselves when you least expect it, we became best friends after watching the movie "Brian's Song". Who would have thought?

Our friendship grew from our playing football together, but the more I got to know Paul, and saw his excellent values demonstrated by the way he lived his life and conducted himself, I continued to be drawn to him. He has never married. I've been married for 47 years. He is introverted. I'm extroverted. He enjoys being by himself. I like going to parties. He is disciplined to the max; I am half-disciplined. We both have our gifts, but they are different. We both love God, but we show it in different ways. When we are together, we discuss how we can improve our lives and be better servants with the talents God has given us.

I can be completely honest with Paul about my failings and he can do the same with me in complete confidence. There's a verse in the Bible that talks about iron sharpens iron. That's what happens when we get together. And although we've always lived a long way from each other, I've always made it a priority to go see him on a regular basis. He does the same with me. We talk on the phone every night, but we never really have deep communication until we're together face-to-face. I always enjoy his company. He is interested in me and encourages me. I do the same for him.

When they were alive, I loved to be around his parents. They were always supporting and encouraging us as long as we stayed within certain parameters. His brother Mark is a true character, much like Will Rogers with a quick wit and a subtle humor. I love being around his brother too. What a great family they have! Choose your friends that have a great family and make them life-long friends. The adventures Paul and I have had over the years would fill a book.

You will be fortunate if you have one Paul in your life. I have been blessed to have many Pauls in my life. Outside of my family, they are my reasons for living. I'll never have much money, but I'm a very wealthy man in term of the life-long friends I've made. I love them and they mean the world to me. They hold me accountable; they encourage me; and they love me in spite of my short comings.

It's a wonderful thing to have friends with godly qualities who want to spend time with you, invest in your life and help you become a better person!

As Shakespeare once wrote, "*A friend is one that knows you as you are, understands where you have been, accepts what you have become, and still, gently allows you to grow.*"

Drugs and Alcohol

Your friends and peers may be your biggest influence when you are a teenager and maybe into your early twenties. Your peer group will affect your decision making much more than you may ever realize, including decisions about drugs and alcohol. Don't ever do illegal drugs and wait until you are 25 to make any decisions about drinking alcohol. One way to protect yourself against addictions is never to start. We have the "additive gene" in our family, so we have to be doubly careful in this area. People who have this addictive gene in them already have one strike against them! Now add the major influence of your peers, and you have a recipe for life-long struggles and sadness if you take the wrong fork in the road.

Grandchildren..... your Grandmother never did illegal drugs, nor did I. Likewise, your Mother never did drugs, nor did your Father. Please follow our example. Illegal drugs only lead to heartache and problems!

I attended a 40-hour training class on drug and alcohol addiction in Baltimore, Maryland, to become a Labor Assistance Professional (LAP) to help my fellow pilots and workers at American Airlines. The course included testimonials, interventions, and videos. It was quite an eye opener for me. Three fourths of our assigned instructors in our training class were in recovery for addiction to drugs and alcohol. They had very, very sad stories about how their addiction recked their families and the lives of the ones they loved. Their experience with drugs and alcohol gave their teaching validity. I got quite an education during that week of intensive training, since I had little experience with drug and alcohol abuse.

The greatest paradigm shift for me resulting from the training was realizing that drug and alcohol addiction, true addiction, is a brain disease. For a true addict, they cannot just say no, nor can they simply make the decision not to drink or not to take drugs. They need specialized help, because it is a brain disease. It's like saying "no" I don't want to have cancer.

Here are some other important facts I learned from that training:

- You can't beat what you don't understand

- When you work with EAP (Employ Assistance Program) or LAP (Labor Assistance Professional), you are in the life-saving business
- Sometimes unknowingly doctors give drugs that actually fuel addiction
- Confidentiality and trust are the keys to working with anyone in rehabilitation. However, confidentiality ends when you are going to hurt yourself or someone else.
- The real key to recovery is in the follow-up
- Why a person becomes addicted to alcohol or drugs is a complex question revolving around hereditary factors, environmental factors, and childhood trauma, which we are also still learning about.
- If you have one parent who was addicted to drugs or alcohol you have a 25% predisposition that you will be addicted. If you have two parents that were addicted to drugs or alcohol, you have a 50% predisposition that you will be addicted to drugs or alcohol.
- As a rule of thumb, the number of years that you have been in addiction equals the number of years you need to be in recovery before you were truly "safe". But for most people, it is a life-long battle that gets easier with time in sobriety.
- As a rule of thumb, you will have between a 40% and 70% success rate if you remain sober with the tools that are given in recovery, and you avoid the triggers that can make you go back to drinking or drugging.
- Being at work and having a job is a great motivator to remain sober. If you are fired from your job or you quit your job you fall into a 30% recovery rate category.
- For alcoholism, you can drink and even have blackout periods and appear completely normal. Women get sicker more quickly than men. A

perfect answer if you were in recovery when you were at a party and someone asks you, "Would you like a drink?" say "Yes, I'll have a Diet Coke on the rocks." That avoids having to say "no" and explain anything.
- Addicts who have been in recovery for five years are now having meltdowns because of COVID. They can't get out of bed and are experiencing depression.
- You have a much higher probability of recovery if there is early intervention, you find a facility with dual diagnosis capability, there is attention paid to trauma-based issues from childhood, and you understand the role and practice the 12-step program.
- If you have a crystal meth problem, there's a 99% probability that you have a sexual addiction problem.
- Detox is a life-threatening event especially if it involves alcohol.
- When you do an intervention, you are threatening to take the most important thing out of that person's life that they care about, and believe they must have.
- The longer you can keep a child from drinking alcohol or taking drugs, the better chance they have a respecting and not abusing those things.
- There is a greater problem with drugs today among youth than alcohol, and each area of the country has a different type of drug that they are dealing with. Testing for what kind of drug the person is on is a very tricky business, because the kids are mixing drugs all the time to get a better high.
- Two Years Ago (2021) 200,000 people overdosed in this country.

As you can see, drugs and alcohol destroy people's lives. But don't think you are different, because they will also destroy your life and the lives of people who love you. If you want to see a graphic illustration of drug addiction, watch the video "Unguarded" by an extremely talented basketball athlete named Chris Herron on ESPN. Finally, if you want to know more about drug and alcohol addiction, there are many books and videos available, at your library or online, that provide invaluable facts and information about these diseases. Please understand how powerful drugs and alcohol are, and how you can become easily addicted given the right circumstances!

Life Lesson #3 — Character — How to Live

Work hard

There are no short cuts in life. It's a fact of life. Work hard and be diligent. Work smart. As I have observed every age group, the ones who have been the happiest and the most successful have been those who have worked hard. Successful people work hard! I've witnessed this fact time and time again

Take my extended family for example. The ones who have worked hard have been the most successful.......in life and in finances. There's no getting around it. You have to work hard or win the lottery. None of my extended family (except one) has won the lottery. And hard work does not necessarily equate to financial success. Sometimes you work hard, very hard, and barely eke out a living. That's okay.

Work is a gift from God. It gives you pleasure most of the time. There's nothing like going to work and working hard all day and coming home and having that feeling that you have accomplished something. The opposite is also true. Sometimes you work hard, very hard and come home frustrated. But over the long run, if you give it your best, work smart and follow your passion, there will be rewards.

This is hard, but the Apostle Paul reminds us to "Work with enthusiasm, as though you were working for the Lord rather than for people."

I knew this guy. You've known him too........never worked hard, didn't study in school, wasn't diligent, always looked for a short cut, never made his bed, never cut the grass, didn't rake the leaves, and was always looking for a "fun" time. He was a little overweight and a lot lazy. He never spent any time learning new skills, much less any time working on his character. He had no mentors. He was like a leaf blowing in the wind. His parents had to support him because he never made quite enough money to pay his bills. Don't be that person! The pattern begins with avoiding hard work and staying in that rut for a long time. You have only yourself to blame. Have fun but be responsible!

Do your best in every phase of life. You can't go back. You have only one life to live. Make the best of it. Plan for the future, but work hard in the moment, applying yourself to every endeavor.

Saint Francis of Assisi once said, *"The only thing ever achieved in life without effort is failure"*.

Develop Personal Discipline

Part of the education here is to learn to say "no" to yourself: self-denial. Developing this trait is key to developing great character! The ability to develop self-discipline and consistently think what is right, say what is right and do what is right, even if you don't want to or you don't feel like it, is one of the greatest marks of genuine maturity.

The trait of personal discipline starts early. This example will shock you. There was a study done at Bing Nursery School on small children in the 70's. It has become known as the Marshmallow Test. For this test they took a single marshmallow and set it in front of the child and told them, "If you don't eat the marshmallow, you will be rewarded by us giving you another marshmallow to eat." The kids were immediately in a quandary. Some of them couldn't resist and ate the first marshmallow right away. Others resisted by not looking at the marshmallow, singing songs, covering their eyes, etc., doing their best to employ deferred gratification. Then the testers tracked these two groups of children as they grew up. What is extremely interesting to me is that the children who held out and exercised self-discipline, even at this early age, when they grew they were in high school scored 210 points higher on the SAT test, were more self-reliant and self-confident, handled pressure better, and in later life had higher incomes, better careers and better marriages on average than the ones who succumbed to self-gratification even at a tender age. Think about this application as you grow up!!

Human nature invites us to be lazy, unthoughtful, mouthy, and physically undisciplined. Resist! Go the other way! Know what is right and force yourself to do it with God's help. Keep yourself within God's parameters, and you will be well ahead of the game.

Think the right thing, say the right thing, and do the right thing.

Think the right thing: The book of Philippians in the 4th Chapter and the 8th Verse could offer no better guidance than you will find anywhere else in the world for your thought life:

> *"And now, dear brothers and sisters, one final thing. Fix your thoughts on what is true, and honorable, and right, and pure, and lovely, and admirable. Think about things that are excellent and worthy of praise."*

Say the right thing: Don't say the first thing that comes into your mind. I'm guilty of that. Develop a filter. Take a breath. Pause and consider how your words will be received by the people you are speaking with. You can't take them back. Words are powerful. The tongue is hard to tame, but you can do it. Be humble. Speak to others as if they were more important than you. Don't be disrespectful.

Teens and now Pre-teens go through a phase when they want to test the limits. When I was young, we only did that once. In most households, the Father of the home made you never forget what disrespect sounded like and looked like. People today say that kind of discipline was too strong. But today, kids push the limits with little or no consequences. It's a fad or a badge of honor to be disrespectful and push the limits. That kind of behavior is championed in our movies and mimicked in our classrooms and finally brought home. It's sad and disheartening to me. Let your words be kind and uplifting or don't speak at all.

The Apostle Paul reminds us to be humble and gentle in Ephesians Chapter 3:2 "Always be humble and gentle. Be patient with each other, making allowance for each other's faults because of your love."

Lastly, do the right thing. The right character is all about putting God first, others second and yourself last. Therefore, developing a Christian godly character is about overcoming your human nature and the desire to put yourself first and satisfy what you want to do when you want to do it! Fighting this nature will last a lifetime. It's like the good angel sitting on one shoulder telling you to do the right thing while the bad angel sits on the other shoulder telling you to do the wrong thing. Chances are, whether the decisions are great or small, you will face this dilemma every day. You have a choice……make the right one!

Lou Holtz said, *"Winners embrace hard work. They love the discipline of it, the trade-off they're making to win. Losers, on the other hand, see it as a punishment. And that's the difference."*

I had a roommate at the Air Force Academy one semester named Steve Duresky. God had given him a lot of gifts and he didn't have to work quite as hard as many cadets did to be successful. But he was a hard worker, and his body was in tip-top shape all the time. After inter-murals he would come up to the room and do extra sit-ups and push-ups. He was the oldest son in the family. I remember one time he went home on Christmas vacation, and after dinner he casually said to his younger brothers who adored him, "Tonight, instead of having ice cream for dessert, I think I'm going to do 25 push-ups." It wasn't long before his brothers were on the floor beside him telling their Mom to skip the ice cream, because they just wanted to have push-ups for dessert! What a great example of leadership and self-discipline.

Developing self-discipline means to deny our selfish desires, to die to our self-centered gratifications, and not respond to every whim of eating, talking, playing computer games, and buying everything in the store. When you see someone start to appropriate this kind of conduct in their lives, you are seeing genuine character being built!

Theodore Roosevelt once said, "With self-discipline, most anything is possible."

Aristotle once said, ""I count him braver who overcomes his desires than him who conquers his enemies; for the hardest victory is over self."

Jim Rohn, an American entrepreneur and philosopher, made it simple when he wrote, "We must all suffer one of two things: the pain of discipline or the pain of regret or disappointment."

Develop self-discipline in your life. It will make all the difference in the world on how you live and succeed. Be organized, measured, and think about your actions.

Follow Your Passion

As a young man or woman growing up, it goes without saying to study hard in school and learn all you can. Learn to think critically, which I will address in the life lesson chapter. Participate in sports, but don't let them dominate your life. Chances are you won't be a professional athlete, but you will be a professional something.

The Bible says in the First Book of Timothy, 4:8 *"Bodily exercise profits little."* You should eat well and do some exercising, but if all you did was to eat smartly and go for walks, you would be very healthy for a long time. You don't have to push your body to the absolute limit. There is so much competition in high school and college today and they play at such a high level in each sport, that you are only doing permanent damage to your body's frame when you play sports beyond the inter-mural level. Even playing inter-murals can be dangerous!

Back to studying hard……Give it your best and learn all you can from your teachers and those around you. Then when you get the chance, follow your passion!

If you want to live and eat, you'll have to get a job and work. Choose something early that you love to do. Work is not work when you love what you are doing. Too many people work to live and not the other way around. And too many people wait too late to pursue their passions. Some never get to their passions in life and that is sad. Find something that gives you job satisfaction.

Denis Waitley once said simply, "Chase your passion, not your pension."

My passion is people, so most of what I have done in life in terms of work has been very satisfying. And I've done a lot of things! Most of my life focused on flying, even though I thought I wanted to be a doctor. I didn't even really know what doctors did or what sacrifices they had to make just to be called a doctor. I couldn't have done a residency, because I need eight hours of sleep and it's really tough for me to stay up for three days in a row!

I'll never forget a young man who worked for me in the Air Force. Jason Woodward was an engineer who loved engineering. He had a beautiful wife and a beautiful baby when Judy and I met them. He dropped out of West Point after one year because West Point and the Army was not for him, even though he was #1 in his class when he left.

He ended up taking a commission in the Air Force and was doing flight test on the T-38 when I met him and his sweet wife. I was a Colonel and he was a young Captain. I wanted to help him be successful in his Air Force career, so I talked to him about being my Executive Officer. There he would learn the ropes about the Air Force much easier and faster than being an engineer, but when he was presented the opportunity, he declined my invitation. I was surprised.

However, when he explained to me his passion for engineering, and how he wanted to be a life-long engineer, my tactic changed. I told him that very few engineers in the Air Force did true engineering, (by in large they managed engineers or engineering projects), so if he really wanted to be an engineer, he should get out of the Air Force. Ultimately, he took my advice and now works for Lockheed Martin as an engineer and an engineering lead. He still doesn't like the "lead" part, but he really enjoys the engineering! His passion is engineering and he discovered it early in life. Not many people are as lucky as this young man.

Bishop T.D. Jakes once said, "If you can't figure out your purpose, figure out your passion. For your passion will lead you right into your purpose."

One more example. My best friend in high school was Billium Beyer. His real name was Bill Beyer, but both he and I couldn't be "Bills", so I named him "Billium". He majored in Math and married a gal named Kyle, whom I love, because she has a kind heart, a sensitive spirit, and she laughs at all my jokes. After college he taught high school math and coached wrestling. Then he became an Air Traffic Controller.

He did well in both these endeavors, but his real passion was working with his hands. Billium can build anything out of wood. He's built one home with little help, and built a large extension on another home where he lives today out in the country.

He also buys small to medium homes in the Kansas City area, remodels them, and then leases or flips them. He owns 22 of them! This is his passion and his ministry. He is able to do something he loves (working with his hands) and provide for his family and his retirement. Plus, he is able to give to others out of the abundance that he has been given by working long and hard.

Follow your heart. Follow your passion. Your life gifts were given to you for a reason. If you use them wisely, you will have so much more impact in life than the person who works at a "job" because he has a nice title, makes a lot of money, or is forced into something due to bad decisions that limited his choices early in life.

The Apostle Paul tells us that each one of us has a special gift. In Ephesians 4:7 he writes, *"However, he has given each one of us a special gift through the generosity of Christ."*

The bottom line comes from Mia Hamm, the professional soccer player who said, "If you don't love what you do, you won't do it with much conviction or passion."

Take care of Your Health

Some people work too hard. If you have your nose to the grindstone all the time, you can run yourself into the ground. My Father-in-Law used to say about engine motors and people, "You only have so many RPMs......Use them wisely!" He was a wise man who knew human nature like no one I've ever known.

I'm concerned about young people's hearing. With all the social media and songs being available that you can listen to with ear buds and ear phones, many times young people turn the volume up too high. You can permanently damage your hearing. When you're young you think that you're invincible, but the older you get, the more you realize how fallible you are!

I've always been a little funny about my dental health and my hearing. I was taught early that your dental health is tied to your heart health. That's a good reason to take care of your teeth and your gums. I've also wanted to have a nice smile and my original teeth when I die. My dental hygiene was not good when I was a small boy, but I've done much better in later life. I'm so glad that I made brushing and flossing a priority.

When I was flying, I always wore double ear protection. My hearing today is better than Judy's (my wife). I am so glad that I protected my hearing when I was young, because music is so enjoyable to me. I just love hearing every note. I can hear conversations across the room. As you grow older, and depending upon your genealogy, you will naturally lose some hearing. I've lost very little. Daddy, my Father-in-Law, used to joke that not being able to hear some things was a blessing, but as I observed him in later life, he was not able to interact in many conversations, because he couldn't hear them. If you do not correct hearing problems within about three years, those tones are gone forever. Daddy was so funny, and for being a man of limited education, he was very wise. Protect your hearing! Good hearing will serve you well in the future.

If you trade your health for wealth, you'll spend all your money and the rest of your life trying to get your health back! I've seen men in the military so intent on making General Officer that they sacrifice their health and their families in a temporal pursuit. You have to find a balance in your life. Pay attention to your health.

We are taught to trust our doctors. After all, they have been to medical school, residency, and are now practicing medicine.....with the emphasis on "practicing". Doctors make mistakes!!! I can't tell you how many times doctors (not intentionally, but regrettably) have made mistakes! One time their inattention to detail almost killed me. Had Judy not been checking on me and my care, I wouldn't be here today! This is also true of her parents and the care they received in Assisted Living. Doctors and medical professionals make mistakes. You need to keep your eye on them and ask questions. Most of the time they are right on the money, but when they make mistakes (they are human), the mistakes could be fatal. Here's what happened to me, that bears repeating, as related in my book "Renegade Colonel":

*** Hospitalized ***

Off and on I tended to get colds. But my colds are not normal – they don't last for two days and then I feel great. My colds go on for over a week and many times result in sinus infections. I think a lot of that is caused by my flying with colds and sinus infections. Because we only flew about once a week in the F-111 I hated to miss a sortie for a cold. So, most of the time I would take a little Afrin and fly. I never got a sinus block but sometimes coming down from altitude I would have trouble clearing my ears. I'm sure that didn't do my sinuses any good.

This particular time I got one of those colds that lasted a week with a tickle in the back of my throat. The chills, fever and cough ended up in a sinus infection and finally I went into the Flight Surgeon and got some antibiotics. He prescribed Bacterium, a sulfa-based drug that he said was particularly effective in clearing up sinus problems. I thanked him and went home to go to bed. I was feeling awful.

Most of the time after just a day or two antibiotics would clear me up. I know what they say about most colds and infections being viral and not responding to antibiotics, but even if mine started out with a viral infection most of the time they developed into a secondary bacterial infection. A lot of doctors (including my friend Rob Sayers) said they didn't help but I knew they did so if I could get antibiotics I would.

However, this time, even after a week I was still feeling awful – much worse than when I started the antibiotics. Feeling miserable I returned to the Flight Surgeon and got another round of antibiotics. He couldn't believe I wasn't feeling better. He told me to go home and rest up drinking plenty of liquids and I would be feeling fine in no time. I took a few doses of the Bacterium following his instructions but I was feeling worse than ever.

I had terrible headaches which were very uncommon for me. I was particularly sensitive to light and noise. When I'm sick I really just like to lay in the bed and be left alone but this time I was reclusive. I just wanted the kids to be quiet and for the lights to be out and for me to be left in silence to suffer. This continued for a few more days and Judy got really concerned as my fever, headaches and chills got worse. She finally said, "I'm taking you to the hospital."

The hospital we used was at the old Mather AFB which had been closed many years after I had attended Nav School there in 1977. However, they kept the hospital open for Reservists and Retired Veterans to use. It was just a few minutes from our house so we zipped over there one night. Judy drove because I was feeling so bad. The doctor did the normal workups not noting anything unusual but the ordinary flu symptoms, but he also included a profile for hepatitis. However, they were concerned with my dehydration (I took three bags of fluid through an IV) and my deceased lung capacity. While there I noticed a friend of mine whom we had been stationed with in Torrejon AB, Spain, Col Corazon David.

I couldn't remember her name but I never forget a face. She was Christian and immediately took oversight of my case. They wanted to keep me in the hospital that night "just for observation". I said that was overkill and asked to go home. Judy being on the conservative side sided with the doctors so I relented and stayed for the night thinking by in the morning I would be fine. After the IVs of fluid, I was already feeling much better and thought my problems were just being dehydrated despite drinking juices and water at home. Col David got me some Demerol for my headaches and that helped also. She was a God-send for both of us but especially Judy.

Judy comes to see me early the next morning and I'm feeling worse again. I just couldn't figure it out. The Demerol only dulled the headaches and the sleeping pill they gave me only provided a couple of hours of sleep. The antibiotics just weren't working or something else is going on. My headaches are approaching migraine level now and I just felt awful. They discuss the idea of sending me to the large medical complex at Travis AFB about an hour down the road. Judy thought that would be a good idea where I could see a specialist.

She didn't have much confidence in these doctors and thinks a specialist could solve the problem. I'm bewildered not knowing what is going on. I just want to feel better. Both the nurses and doctors argue for keeping me right there. They conclude that I would get more specialized attention at their smaller hospital, there is a good risk of encountering some other kind of infection in those larger medical facilities, and it would be harder for Judy to see me having to commute for over an hour to get there. They say in a large medical facility sometimes you get lost in the system. At this point my lungs have some fluid in them and they've diagnosed me with pneumonia. This was the third time in my life to have a major case of pneumonia. Judy and I conclude their arguments make sense and we are comfortable with staying right there near home.

I don't rest well that day and hardly sleep that night. When Judy sees me the next morning I am laying in a fetal position on the bed and she senses something is drastically wrong. The doctors ask to meet with her and tell her they are transferring me to Travis AFB immediately. "No, no she said. I'm comfortable with you all taking care of him right here." Then they say in a solemn tone, "Ma'am we're past that point right now. His lungs are shutting down and he may not make it. We don't know what is happening but the situation is grave. We've called an ambulance.

You need to call the lawyers on base and get a general power of attorney right away so you will be in control of all your assets and be able to make decisions for him from here on out. We aren't sure how long he will maintain consciousness." Judy is in shock. I'm only partially aware of what is going on because I feel so bad. The medical technicians are taking my vital signs every 15 minutes. My headaches are unbearable, I'm sensitive to the light, and I'm having trouble breathing – generally speaking I'm feeling really bad.

The lawyers draw up the papers right away – Judy makes arrangements for someone to watch Evie and I'm loaded into the ambulance. Ted and Mitsi who had watched our dog Baby while we were in Hawaii take her again. Judy plans to follow the ambulance in our car. My Brother-in-Law, Tony made reservations for her to stay in the Fisher House on Travis AFB – a really nice big home on base where families of terminal cancer patients can stay at no cost. She was so thankful for the support people are giving her.

I'm semi-conscious as we drive down to Travis AFB. I'm having a really hard time breathing despite being hooked up to oxygen. When we pull in the ambulance entrance to the hospital Judy jumps out of the car to check on me. I tell her I can hardly breathe and that's when she notices the oxygen has not been turned on! She brings it to the attention of the Medical Technician and they are embarrassed and turn on the oxygen right away. Immediately I feel relief.

They wheel me up into the emergency room and I've taken to the back right away where they begin several tests to diagnose what is going on. I'm put into intensive care but the results of all the blood work and lab work show nothing but normal flu symptoms. The first night is rough but they slowly begin to stop the lungs from shutting down by pumping liquid antibiotics into me bag after bag.

My temperature comes down a little but I'm still feeling pretty bad. They release me from intensive care after a couple of days and put me on a floor with terminal patients. All the people with me are old. I'm thinking I'm on the wrong floor. There is mass confusion of the floor – people running everywhere, Code Blues and a shortage of personnel.

My roommate was a man about 81 named Mr. Lyons who was in critical condition due to bleeding in the brain. His body was rejecting the platelets that he was being given so they couldn't operate on him. He refused to cooperate with the nursing and doctor staff and he didn't have a family. I feel really sorry for the gentleman. They come in and ask him the same questions every day. "What day of the week is it? "How old are you?" "Who is the President? – really simple questions. I could tell he was irritated by them and sometimes he would give them the wrong answers intentionally just to work them up.

Mr. Lyons was funny. One night this little medical technician who could hardly speak English comes in and asked Mr. Lyons how old he was. Contributing to the confusion was the fact that Mr. Lyons was hard of hearing. He thought that she was asking him how old <u>she</u> was! He said, "Honey, I have no idea how old you are." She said, "No, no, how old are you?" Again, he gets it backward and this goes on for a few minutes. It reminded me of the comic routine "Who's On First?" He provided some comic entertainment in a not-so-funny place.

As I talk with him I discover he is not a Christian. I found out that he was an old Navy submariner and had worked for Westinghouse after military retirement. Then I shared the gospel with him knowing he didn't have long to live. I had an overwhelming sense that the Lord wanted me to talk with him about salvation. Before saying anything I had prayed that Mr. Lyon's heart would be prepared for what the Holy Spirit had for him that day. It was completely amazing given his previous confusion that we had perfect communication.

He seemed to be hearing better, had good understanding, had no coughing spells like he had before, and we only had one brief interruption in the 15 minutes we talked. I said that through the week I had heard him use the Lord's name in vain several times and that I perceived he wasn't a church going man. He said yes that was right. Then I asked him if he were to die, did he know where he was going. He again understood and seemed to indicate that although he was baptized as a child he wasn't going to heaven and would be cremated.

I explained the gospel briefly by saying that all men have sinned (and he acknowledged his own sin), that we were required to confess our sins to God, and that He would forgive our sins based upon his death on the cross, and that if we asked Jesus into our hearts, that He was waiting to come in and prepare a place for us with Him in heaven. I asked Mr. Lyons if that concept was ever explained to him and if he understood what I was saying. He said he understood the concept even as a child but he was only going through the motions so he knew it was not a real conversion.

Then I asked if he would like to confess his sin to God and receive Jesus Christ into his heart right then. I'll never forget his response. "No, I don't believe I want to do that." I said, "Mr. Lyons this seems like a no-brainer. You don't have long to live and you're being given the choice between everlasting life with God or spending the rest of eternity in everlasting torment, burning and gnashing of teeth eternally separated from God." He said he understood but he just did not want to make the decision right now. Knowing it is the Holy Spirit that does the convicting and convincing, I left it at that having been obedient to God with my responsibility to Mr. Lyons as I understood it. I told him that I would be praying for him and urged him to receive Jesus into his heart. He said he would be thinking about it.

Eventually he was moved to a skilled nursing facility when his condition worsened and he refused his oral antibiotics and kept pulling out his oxygen. Unfortunately, after I was discharged he passed away. I pray that he came to peace with God before he died.

Shortly after I got up there to the floor Judy noticed that one of my IVs was not dripping. She called the nurses attention to it and they got it fixed right away. I was fortunate she was with me. What they told us down at Mather was coming true – you just didn't get the individualized attention in a large medical facility. They were taking blood from me all the time.

My veins were collapsing making it difficult to get a good "stick". My veins are small anyway. I asked for the "A" Team so they could hit the vein the first time. Even with the people up there who did transfusions they were having problems hitting my small veins. I asked if possibly they could put a port in my leg. They said, "Sure". However, when the technician was getting set up he dropped the needle on the floor. I thought I should have said something but I was feeling so bad I didn't say anything. I was just glad they were not sticking my arms. My body was swelling up for some reason. My weight was 220 lbs. when I was admitted and after a few days I was weighing 247 lbs. My hands and feet looked bloated.

My right knee and right ankle swelled to about twice their normal size. Then Judy lifts my hospital gown to compare the size of my legs. All the sudden she notices a red streak running from my IV up my leg to my knee. She calls the nurse again who immediately summons a doctor. I had a staph infection – if it would have climbed up my vein much further it would have gone to my heart and killed me. Again, I was thankful she was there. She also helped my roommate Mr. Lyons when he couldn't breathe. She was always helping the medical technicians or nurses with something. She was and is invaluable to me.

Eventually they got my headaches and fever under control. I still wasn't doing well. One morning I woke up and my knee was the size of a balloon. I didn't remember hitting it on anything but I was on so much pain medication

I thought I might have gotten it stuck in the bed at night and twisted in without realizing what had happened. Anyway, before anything else happened to me the doctors decided to discharge me on crutches and get the knee taken care of back at the Mather hospital.

I went in for an orthopedic consult the day after we got home and they pulled 40 cc's of fluid off my right knee and said to continue with the crutches. They confirmed there wasn't an infection in there. I eventually regained full motion of the knee and got my strength back but not until I had three weeks of convalescent leave. I had always wanted to grow a beard but Judy didn't want me to.

This time she relented and during my recovery I would walk around the block with my old friend Ted. He and I would talk about everything as we sauntered along. He was a good companion and I think he liked me being at home. Eventually I gained most of my strength back, shaved and returned to work. They never did figure out what the cause of my illness was until a year later just by accident. Here's how I recorded what happened back in 1998 when I wrote an article so the same thing wouldn't happen to someone else like it did to me:

It's hard to be thankful for being sick, but this time I was – the circumstances of this illness answered the mystery of the succession of my flu, pneumonia, pulmonary failure, staph infection and near death in January 1998. What I learned from this may be of value to you or some of your loved ones. That's why I want to share it with you. If you're a doctor, please don't hold me accountable for the technical medical terms. This story is told strictly from a layman's perspective.

My symptoms began very similarly to last year's flu with a plane flight back from Dayton. I got a head cold picking up some germ on the airplane, I suspect. After a couple *of days of continually blowing my nose, I tried to fight it off with a simple decongestant. However, after a couple of weeks of sniffling around, being on the verge of a sinus infection, and feeling about 75%, I went in to see the flight surgeon for some antibiotics to knock it out once and for all.*

The flight surgeon prescribed Bacterium, a sulfa-based anti-biotic known for its great success combating sinus infections. I took one pill Monday morning after my visit to the doctors with complete confidence I would be on the mend by Tuesday. But, by Monday at noon I felt worse than ever. I had a headache, sinus pain, chills, fever, joint aches, and generally felt like I had a bad case of the flu.

I went home, telling my secretary that I was sure I would be back in the office the next morning. However, Tuesday morning I felt worse than ever. I had a terrible night's sleep experiencing the same symptoms I described, only in greater intensity. In fact, I thought, this is awful, "I feel just like I did in January 1998. I can remember these feelings as plain as day. I don't want this to develop into pneumonia again and have to make a return visit to the hospital."

Convincing myself that if I didn't feel any better Wednesday morning that I was returning to the flight surgeon, I attempted to go to sleep Tuesday night. Well, I had the same kind of awful night tossing and turning, and felt even worse Wednesday morning. I took one more pill of the Bacterium and called the flight surgeon.

As God's Providence would have it, he was scheduled to fly that day. Next I called a doctor friend of ours who oversaw my care the last time I was in the hospital, but she was at a medical conference in San Francisco. Then I thought about the doctor who had admitted me to the hospital nearly a year and a half ago, who was familiar with my case. Although he worked in primary care, he agreed to see me if I could make it in by 1:15 PM. My wife zoomed me up to the hospital.

When he saw me, he said, "Boy, sir, you look like death warmed over! Is this de ja vue?" I said I wasn't sure, but he had to do something. I felt like I had been down this road before, and it wasn't a pleasant journey. I told him I had the same old symptoms as last time – severe headache, chills, fever (despite taking 800mg of Motrin three times per day), and my body ached all over. It even hurt to lie down. My eyes were sensitive to the light, and any kind of noise bothered me.

He said, "Wait just one second, while I research your record." Then this wise physician discovered the problem. He said, "Did you realize that you were on Bacterium the last time you were sick? I think you're having an adverse reaction to the Bacterium. I'm changing you over to Amoxicillin and Augmentin, and if you're not better in two days, come back and see me. I'm treating a patient right now that I've given Bacterium, and she is experiencing sores all in her mouth, and severe pain in her joints."

And that was it. Within a day, I was feeling noticeably better. I also learned that Evelyn, my daughter, is allergic to Bacterium and breaks out into a severe rash, when she takes it. I was so happy to solve the mystery of what triggered my descending series of events in January 1998 (They tested for Hepatitis A, B, and C, spinal meningitis, and several other diseases, all with negative results), and to be relieved of the pain I was in!

Even though I did not have a classic "allergic" reaction to the antibiotic, the lesson learned for me is that if the medication is not working as advertised, or if you are not making normal progress, you might suspect the medication itself! As I've told this to many people, I've heard stories of people having many side effects from medication to include death from adverse reactions to the medication itself. Most of the time medicines are great aids to the healing process; other times they can actually worsen the original condition. You need to be sensitive to your own body's reaction to drugs, even ones uniquely designed to combat your illness. It could save your life someday.

For men you have to do two things with regard to your health as you approach 50.......sooner if you have a history of poor health in these areas. Get your PSA test every year, and get regular colonoscopies. It's easy......just another lab test from your normal blood draw during your annual physical. We had to get annual physicals in the Air Force, but if you don't have that forcing function, develop the discipline to get an annual physical no matter how you feel. The other test you must get is a colonoscopy. Again, not a difficult test.......the prep is a little messy, but not nearly as messy as colon cancer!

I had a good buddy I used to fly with in F-111's. His name was Beau Lucas. He was smart, funny, an excellent Weapon Systems Officer (WSO), and he loved to fly jets. Due to some unusual circumstances about mid-career, he got out of the Air Force and took over his father's commercial real estate company in Dallas. He made a lot of money......much more than he would have made staying in the Air Force, but I used to tease him that I had more fun!

I actually got forced out of the Air Force shortly after Beau left the Air Force. I also ended up in Dallas living with my in-laws and looking for a real job. Beau was so kind and compassionate offering me a job, if my other pursuits in the defense industrial complex working for a major contractor didn't pan out. I'll always remember his kindness for the rest of my life when I was down and needed to generate some income to take care of my wife and two small daughters.

Beau worked hard. He worked long hours and he knew his trade. He was richly rewarded for doing a great job every day, and when he left the Air Force it was a tight market and one of his competitors was Roger Staubach in the commercial real estate market.

To make a long story short, Beau never got a colonoscopy until he was 60 years old when he had symptoms. It was too late. He was diagnosed with Stage 4 colon cancer. There's little you can do at that point. Yes, he went through all the terrible protocols including many rounds of chemotherapy, but nothing ever really worked. It didn't have to be that way. I walked the last stage of his life with him and was there with many of his F-111 buddies at his memorial. We couldn't believe it. He left us far too early!

I've told some close friends and family if I had to do it again, I wouldn't have played Division I college football. It was just too hard on my body and all my opponents were bigger and stronger than I was. Generally speaking, I was faster than they were, but speed will only take you so far when you're a defensive end and Notre Dame calls the play "Student Body Left"! The first people you meet are the two pulling guards (about 6'5" and 300 lbs. each and strong), followed by the toughest, meanest fullback in history (my size at 6'2" and 240 lbs.) and then you have to find the All-American half back and try to make the tackle!

I got beat up game after game. It took a toll on my body and I'm feeling it today in my shoulders, knees and ankles at 70 years old. I'd still be a great athlete if I wouldn't have played that level of football, lacrosse and wrestling at the Academy. And then I played Class A racquetball and did further damage to my back (in addition to flying fighters) that I didn't have to do. It was a choice I made when I was young, because I was such a fierce competitor. I regret it today, despite all the wonderful friends I made on the grid iron, and all the wonderful experiences and travel I did while in college.

You don't have to be a runner. You don't have to push yourself to the max in lifting weights. You don't have to beat your body up. Just keep in shape. Do some cardio exercises and stay tone. Spend your effort in developing your character! Invest your life in the lives of others! Prioritize what really matters in life!

And don't let yourself get overweight......either through self-indulgence or thyroid problems or slow metabolism or whatever. Weight is far easier to put on than to take and keep off......believe me! For each year after you turn 60, you need 1% less intake of calories to maintain the same weight. When you're young, it's hard to gain weight, but when you get older, not so hard. I used to take a gallon of milk and a dozen cookies to try to gain weight after dinner at the Air Force Academy, but I was burning so many calories, I would not gain an ounce!

Being obese causes all kinds of health problems. Hopefully when you are young, your parents will be able to serve you healthy food and make sure you develop good eating habits that don't include too much sugar. Being grossly overweight can affect your self-image. It will affect your confidence in most cases, which might lead to greater health problems. It's a vicious downward spiral. Take care of your health. Your body is the temple of the Holy Spirit.

Shakespeare once wrote "Our bodies are our gardens—our wills are our gardeners."

Planning, Preparation and Execution

Without a vision, the people perish
Proverbs 29:18

Planning, preparation, and execution are some of the important keys to success. We need to be organized and prioritize important tasks before executing them. Establish purpose, direction, priorities, and then act or present!

Successful speakers have outlines and know what message they want to deliver through humor or examples or emphasis. In my first speech in high school as a sophomore, I was paralyzed, spoke much louder than I thought I did, and the kids laughed when I was done. I felt horrible. I continued to work on my delivery. My speeches got better as I studied people who did it best, and my confidence grew. Now, I can deliver a talk without even thinking about being scared. I put my emphasis on what message I want the audience to receive, but also what is the best way to deliver that message.

The same is true for so many things in life. You have to do your homework! Knowledge is power. Lawyers know this better than anyone. If you want a project to be successful, there are three main ingredients: product, process, and people. But the most important ingredient is the people. If you don't have talented or motivated people, you will never have a successful team! Entire college courses are dedicated to this subject, and you can get a certification in this discipline, but it will always boil down to product, process, and people.

Will Rogers once said: *"Plans get you into things but you've got to work your way out."* He also said, *"A vision, without a plan, is just a hallucination."*

Pay attention to the Details

Details make perfection, and perfection is not a detail.

Leonardo Da Vinci

Paul Hansen, my best friend from Oregon, had an unbelievable father. His dad once told him, "Pay attention to the small change, and the dollars will take care of themselves." It works with money and it works in life. Pay attention to the small things. They matter!

I have to admit, I'm not great at this. I'm a big picture guy. I don't like the details. I like to have people who work for me take care of the details. I'm an "ideas" guy. I like to develop the vision. I naturally see the big picture. I see the forest from the trees without even trying. It's a gift, but it's also a burden, because I have to work extra hard on being more aware of the small things.

Paying attention to the details is often what separates the winners from the losers. You see this most clearly in the court room. Every detail matters there. Lawyers are studious. They read reams of background information, whittle it down, and bring the pertinent facts to court. The ones who put the time and effort into preparations are normally the ones who win in court. That's why most public defenders are terrible; they just aren't paid enough to put in the time needed to win!

Most of life is filled with ordinary days, not a lot of drama, no big events. But, it is on those ordinary days, and what you do with those days that makes your big days a success or failure. Be disciplined. We've talked about that earlier. Being faithful in little things will make you successful in the big things.

In life, character and time are very important. You must prioritize your time (make a schedule) and work at developing your character. The best way to prepare for tomorrow is to do your best today. Spend time with God alone. He talks to you in many ways, including the Bible. LISTEN! We've talked about spending time with your mentors. Seize the day; seize the moment. Use those ordinary days wisely. Don't get ahead of yourself.

I once had a young Captain working for me. His name was Bob (not his real name). He was bright and wanted to go to Test Pilot School. I didn't know him very well, because he worked in a large group of military and civilian engineers and I was new to the organization. He approached me and said that he wanted to go to Test Pilot School. It had been his dream ever since he was a young man. I listened to him carefully and told him I would get back to him shortly.

I went to his supervisor and said, "Tell me about Bob. What kind of engineer is he? What kind of person is he? How are his technical skills? What kind of reputation does he have in the Group?" Well, to make a long story short, Glen had a poor reputation because he was a slacker. He took on the projects he was interested in, but when there was real work to do, he disappeared. He left early on Fridays for the weekend. You could never count on him.

I called Bob to my office the next week and told him what I had discovered about his work ethic and his character. I told him that I admired him for wanting to go to Test Pilot School, and his supervisor felt he had the basic tools to get there, but given his performance, I would never endorse him to go to that prestigious school.

I also told him that this conversation would be kept private between the two of us, and that he could control his destiny. He was a young officer, and with lots of hard work, listening carefully to those above him, and applying himself to every situation, he could change his reputation. He could become known as someone who stayed late, if need be, someone who took on the tough projects and could be counted on to show up. Bottom line was that if he was not impressing his supervisor, he would never impress me or get my backing to go to Test Pilot School. That was not an easy thing to say.

Telling someone about their weaknesses never is, but a good supervisor and mentor finds a way to do it.

I'm happy to report that this young officer took my advice to the core. It was like night and day for the next year on how he conducted himself. I followed up with his supervisor and made trips now and then down to his group to see how his was doing. He was working hard and he was more content in his work and in his career supporting A-10 operations. After some time, I wrote him a strong letter of recommendation to attend Test Pilot School! He met the Board and was selected shortly thereafter.

He was assigned to Edward AFB, graduated with honors and went on to have a very successful Air Force career. His ordinary days and his boring projects prepared him for greater things as he paid attention to detail and kept track of the small things. He didn't procrastinate. He made the most of his circumstances. He made a 180 degree turn and it turned his life around!

> *It's the little details that are vital. Little things make big things happen."*
> *John Wooden, Basketball Coach*
>
> *Details matter. It's worth waiting to get it right.*
> *Seve Jobs, Founder of Apple*
>
> *If you place the emphasis on getting the little things right, and address the everyday problems that come up, you can encourage a culture of attention to detail.*
> *Richard Branson, Founder of Virgin Airlines*

Pursue maturity

Perfection is not attainable, but if we chase perfection, we can catch excellence.
Vince Lombardi

Mature people think about choices and consequences. The Bible uses the word "perfection" when talking about maturity. We are encouraged to be perfect as Jesus is perfect. We are to follow and imitate Christ. However, it is important to understand that Jesus is not saying that we have to be "perfect." He is saying we must pursue maturity in all areas of our life. It will not always be fun, but it will provide a deep sense of satisfaction. Act, dress and be dignified and professional. If you do, people will have confidence in you. Don't do everything out of spontaneity; think about your choices and consequences. But don't forget to have a little safe fun along the way!

When you do Wrong

In the previous section, I mentioned working toward perfection, but everyone fails. When you sin, you are falling short of the glory of God. It's violating or not listening to your conscience. Sin begins in the mind. The best way to battle sin and win is when sin first enters your mind, not after you commit the act. Do not let sin dwell in your mind or have time to cultivate into something else.

If you give sin time and opportunity, it will come out in your speech and your actions. It will happen during your life, and when it happens, humble yourself before God; confess your sin, and ask God to forgive you. Be sincere and stop sinning. Then pull yourself up, put your face to the wind, and start moving again. Don't rationalize your sin. Don't minimize your sin. Don't make excuses. Face your sin head on and ask for forgiveness. Then look forward and move forward.

I don't like to talk about sin, especially my sins, so let's move on!

Don't follow the Crowd

Only dead fish go with the flow!
Unknown

When you follow the crowd, it may be going where you want to go, but then again it may not! Don't be a "Wanna Be"! Be yourself and have confidence in yourself. You were made by God for a specific purpose. You have gifts and talents that you need to use. Follow your gut. Be a man or a woman of courage! Surround yourself with the right people who are making the right decisions for the right reasons. People who immerse themselves in drinking and drugs are not the people you want to associate with. You are unique. Find out what you are good at, and then hone that skill set. It will take work, but you will be rewarded in time.

I have a Godson named Jacob Woodward. He's Jacob Woodward son that I mentioned earlier. I am so proud of him. When he was just a little guy, but he loved to make little characters out of Legos and pretend he was making a movie. He continued to dream. Soon he was taking pictures of his little characters with a camera. Then he borrowed his dad's iPhone and found out how to make them move, and he made a little movie with a little background set that he also constructed. He loved making these little simple movies. It was his passion.

He went to a Catholic grade school, and then he was homeschooled for high school. All during this time, he continued to make his little movies. When it came time to go to university, he didn't consider Norte Dame or

Yale or Harvard or Stanford. Instead, he looked for a college that specialized in making movies so he could learn the trade of producing movies. He ended up going to John Paul in Escondido, California.

Today he is working on producing a Christian movie that will influence many people, possibly many thousands of people. You will never know where little Jacob will end up, because he did not follow the crowd. He followed his heart and became better at what he loved to do!

Albert Einstein once wrote, *"The one who follows the crowd will usually go no further than the crowd. Those who walk alone are likely to find themselves in places no one has ever been before."*

> *Often, problems are knots with many strands, and looking at those strands can make a problem seem different*
>
> Mr. Rogers

One of the best ways to avoid being controlled by your emotions and entering into failure is to avoid bad situations. Temptations are out there and they are many. Science and marketing have been perfected so that, together, they can easily manipulate your desires if you are not careful. It's called advertising!

We know that over-eating is bad for us. In fact, anything not done in moderation is generally bad. Sitting down and eating a big bag of potato chips or a whole carton of ice cream or a whole bag of chocolates is not good for you. But sometimes as I've said, "It's hard to find a stopping place!"

That's food, and the manufacturers of food have targeted our taste buds so they know exactly what we crave. And if you only indulge once or twice then no harm is done. However, if you can't stop eating or drinking excessively, it could end in premature death. But there are greater temptations that can also lead to death. How many times do I have to say don't try drugs and alcohol to drive home the point? Just avoid them. There used to be a slogan saying, "Just say no!" Now Nike has a slogan saying "Just do it!" You have choices and choices have consequences!

I remember when I was 16 and I had just gotten my driver's license. A couple of my friends were in the car and we were coming back from an outdoor musical in Kansas City. There was a long stretch of highway that was practically all downhill. I said to my buddies, "Let's see how fast we can get this old Ford to go. Do you think it will do 100 mph downhill?" Do you think that was a good idea? Do you think anyone in the car said, "Bill, let's not do this! That's not a good idea! This old car may fall apart. One of the wheels may come off. We may get in a wreck. The engine might blow up. We may kill someone else besides ourselves if something goes wrong at that high speed!" No, we just did it, and fortunately nothing bad happened, but that's not always the case. God saved me from the error of my ways that time. Some have said my Guardian Angel gets paid overtime!

Flee from bad situations that lead to temptations! Sometimes you just have to get out of a situation you know in your gut just isn't right. No doubt you'll be invited to a party or a gathering of your peers one day, and immediately you'll know that's not the place for you. But, you won't want to be embarrassed by leaving as soon as you got there. Maybe you would have to call your mom or dad to come get you. You won't want to draw attention to yourself, but this is a time that happens in most teenagers' lives, where you have to be strong. You have to make the right decision. You have to listen to your conscience. Staying there, even though you don't partake in what's going on, could have some very negative consequences for you. Get out of there! Leave right away. Get home and call Grandpa! I'll be the first one to tell you how proud I am of you that you did the right thing in the face of peer pressure. I will applaud you and reward you!

<u>Be Responsible</u>

Responsibility is the price of greatness
Winston Churchill

Nothing good happens without serious effort, commitment, discipline and perseverance. Success in life begins with the simple things. When you wake up, thank God for letting you wake up. Brush your teeth (and do a good job). Be responsible in the little tasks. Dental health is important not only for your teeth and gums, but believe it or not for your heart as well! Wash your face. Get ready for the day. Make your bed. Build discipline into your life. Build good habits over a lifetime.

Warren Buffett, one of the richest persons in the world, an American business magnate, investor, speaker and philanthropist, said "No matter how great the talent or efforts, some things just take time. You can't produce a baby in one month by getting nine women pregnant."

These seem like little things, but little things, over time, pay great dividends. It's like saving money. If you can, save 10% of your earnings, but even if you save less, just save. If you saved $400 a month over a 40-year working life, you would have $1.5M in savings, based on nominal returns on investments. Saving is hard, especially when you're young, but saving and investing is a must!

Some people are morning people and some people are night owls. I don't know why, but they both need discipline. Don't fight your tendencies, but if you are not a morning person it will be much harder to face the morning tasks. If you are not a night owl, it will be harder to stay up and finish that assignment, to brush your teeth when you're tired, to say your prayers and thank God for the day, and to say prayers for others that need them for the next day.

Keep a clean room! Cleanliness is close to godliness. Be an organized person. Be respectful. Be polite. Use your manners. It matters! You are developing life-long habits that define your character. Be responsible! As Honest Abe once said, *"You can't escape the responsibility of tomorrow by evading it today."*

Take a lesson from the Marines

Semper Fidelis – Be Faithful & Loyal

"Great is Thy Faithfulness"

One of my favorite hymns!

Great is Thy faithfulness, O God my Father
There is no shadow of turning with Thee
Thou changest not, Thy compassions, they fail not
As Thou hast been, Thou forever will be

Great is Thy faithfulness
Great is Thy faithfulness
Morning by morning new mercies I see
All I have needed Thy hand hath provided
Great is Thy faithfulness, Lord, unto me

Summer and winter and springtime and harvest
Sun, moon and stars in their courses above
Join with all nature in manifold witness
To Thy great faithfulness, mercy and love

Great is Thy faithfulness

Great is Thy faithfulness
Morning by morning new mercies I see
All I have needed Thy hand hath provided
Great is Thy faithfulness, Lord, unto me

Pardon for sin and a peace that endureth
Thine own dear presence to cheer and to guide
Strength for today and bright hope for tomorrow
Blessings all mine with 10, 000 beside

Great is Thy faithfulness
Great is Thy faithfulness
Morning by morning new mercies I see
All I have needed Thy hand hath provided
Great is Thy faithfulness
Great is Thy faithfulness
Great is Thy faithfulness, Lord, unto me

Semper Fi - Always Faithful! Be a faithful person. Be a man or woman of your word! Be trustworthy. Always do what is right. The person who is faithful in small things is faithful in big things! Discipline yourself to be faithful and not self-indulgent.

Don't let your eyes wander. In the military we used to say, "Cage your eyes Mister!" Not a bad lesson. Remember what happened to King David. He let his eyes wander over to Bathsheba. The rest of the story was disaster for a man after God's own heart.

Wrong thinking, wrong feeling, wrong doing can take anyone down. Don't get near the line you are not supposed to cross. Don't commit the big errors and chances are you won't suffer big consequences. Where is the line that you are not supposed to cross? Don't worry about it, your conscience will let you know about it. God gave you a conscience, so listen to your gut.

I've been teaching a guy to play golf for the last four years. Jason Espinoza is his name. He's a banker and always wanted to learn how to play golf. He made it one of his goals to learn how to play golf, so he could play in the local tournaments and maybe do some business on the golf course, which is a great idea!

We met at a social gathering. I had a nice golf shirt on and he approached me and asked whether I was a pro golfer or not. Hardly I replied! But I told him if he wanted to learn the basics of golf, I could get him started. So, that is what began a four-year friendship and Jason learning the fundamentals of golf.

As I have observed Jason, who just turned 39, in his job as a banker, he is very focused and detail-oriented. He dresses professionally, is on time, is pleasant and knows the ins and outs of business loans. All the skills he develops and improves on make him a better person and a better golfer. He is disciplined. He is going somewhere. During our friendship he moved out of an apartment and bought his first home for an investment.

Just recently, he was promoted to Assistant Vice President of his bank. He works hard to meet his goals, is loyal to his boss, his customers, and his bank. He is a man of his word. He is also a Christian. I enjoy getting together with Jason as we talk about golf and life. It encourages me to see a young man that has a vision. He reminds me of my Son-in-Laws. I've encouraged him to find another golf instructor who can take his game to the next level, but he says that he is comfortable with me.

I started this section with the title of one of my favorite hymns, "Great is Thy Faithfulness". No one is more faithful than God! I believe that so much that I've requested that this specific hymn be sung at my funeral. Being faithful is a goal worth pursuing!

Be Teachable

I am the wisest man alive, for I know one thing, and that is that I know nothing
                                                            Socrates

Have the humility to know you don't know it all...that comes with age. Ironically, the more you know, the more you realize you don't know it all. There's a big world out there full of adventures, people, and scenery that will astound you! Learn how to read (that is a great Life Lesson in itself) and then read great books. Read the Classics!

Developing a good character begins with the knowledge of knowing what is good and what is not so good. Remember, everyone learns, some learn the hard way and some learn the easy way, but everyone learns in the end. Learn from others' experiences and mistakes, so you won't have to experience unpleasant things brought on by your own wrong choices.

Reading will ultimately be a time saver for you. If you can learn from the stories of others, you will do it right the first time. Many people today use YouTube to see how things are put together, how things are repaired, and how things are restored. There's a lot of great information on the internet to save you time and money.

Always be preparing yourself for the next phase of your life. Weigh your options. Greg Laurie, one of my favorite Pastors in California, once said, *"Heaven is a prepared place for a prepared people"*. That is a profound statement!

Unlike my generation, young people today change jobs and careers at the drop of a hat. Keep your resume updated and always be open to new opportunities that might be presented to you. You can never tell when God will close a door and open a window. When my job position was eliminated from Lockheed Martin, I thought it was the end of my life. Little did I know that God was providing me a job of a lifetime at American Airlines, even though I started at 25% of the salary that I was making at Lockheed Martin!

Be a life-long learner! It's good for your mind, and it's good for your life. I'm always amazed at how my classmates from the AF Academy continue to learn after graduating from the Academy or retiring from the Air Force! Almost everyone got a Master's Degree (including me) because it used to be required to make Major in the Air Force. In fact, many continued to the PhD level! I believe the #1 post-education degree from Academy Graduates is a law degree.

Whether you continue in a formal education program, or a skill set, or a craft or a hobby, be a life-long learner. Don't be satisfied going to work and coming home and watching the television and drinking beer!

Will Rogers once said, "There are three kinds of men. The one that learns by reading. The few who learn by observation. The rest of them have to pee on the electric fence for themselves."

Don't be one of those guys!!!

Be an Encourager!

The pen is mightier than the sword
Edward Bulwer-Lytton

Everyone needs validation and everyone likes to be sincerely complimented. Be an encourager, but especially encourage those who are trying to do right. Don't waste a lot of time on the fools of life. Time is a gift and you only have so much time in a day.

The Book of Proverbs has a lot to say about the tongue, good and bad. Words are powerful. Use them wisely. Whoever keeps his language right and his tongue from lying keeps his soul from trouble. A wholesome tongue is the tree of life. Learn the lessons of speaking rightly. You can crush someone with your words, or you can encourage someone with your words. They are powerful.

There are 31 chapters in the Book of Proverbs. Some people have been diligent enough to read one chapter each day for a month year after year. Your mind is like a computer, good input equals good output. The opposite is also true......garbage in, garbage out.

Your choice of words and comparisons can have a lasting impact on someone's life. Words such as warrior, a "cut above", smart, hard worker, sharper than an axe, courageous, and even comparing folks to people in the Bible, create images in their minds. If you're sincere and repeat those compliments, your words will leave a vision and an impact that far exceeds your expectation or your understanding! And it costs nothing to encourage someone!

One of the best, most powerful encouragers I ever knew was one of my life-time mentors, James Jeffrey. He was such a powerful encourager that you just loved to be in his presence. Whenever I came to see him, he would jump up from behind his desk and say, "Hey, Bill Murray! You've just made my day! How are you? You look great! Get over here and let me feel those arms! You've been lifting weights again you strong guy! How did you get so handsome and strong all at the same time!" And he would say it with such sincerity and enthusiasm that I couldn't drink it in fast enough!

Jeff was a story teller and a great public speaker. He was the best public speaker I've ever heard, easily in the category of Lou Holtz or Tony Robbins. His stories always had a lesson in them. I remember them to this day. Jeff died in 1991 from pancreatic cancer. I still miss him. He was in a league of his own. He was my close friend and life-time mentor....There will never be another Jeff. God broke the mold when He made Jeff!

Here's an excerpt from my book "Renegade Colonel" about Jeff. I loved the way he would encourage me:

I can still recall many of Jeff's talks – Slop Bucket Repentance is one I'll never forget. He told the story of the Prodigal Son in the Bible and then put a modern-day spin on it portraying how in repentance we really don't come clean today – we bring a little slop (sin) back to the farmhouse with us and hide it in the closet just in case we wanted to go back to it. He had so many great stories and illustrations it's hard to remember them all.

Another one that resonated with me was – If the Yarn Gets Tangled, Call the Master – a story about a machine operator who tried to fix the spinning machine after getting a little tangle, but by the time he called for help there was such a mess it would take weeks to solve the problem – an illustration to us to repent at the very first sign of trouble and not dig ourselves a bigger hole by trying to cover things up.

He always read the children's story of the Velveteen Rabbit by Margery Williams originally published in 1922– one of my very favorite books in all the world, talking about being a real person with real qualities. The way Jeff read the story and explained the meaning to these big husky football players was unbelievable. He could bring us to tears every time by the end of the story. We knew in our hearts what he was telling us was right. To be Christians and men of character, we had to be real. Jeff was my friend – a highly valued friend. He used to share a poem about friendship with us. I'm not sure who wrote it.

Portrait of a Friend

When things don't go right, he comes right in.
When none of your dreams come true, he is.
He never looks for your money except when you've lost it. Nothing is more important to him than making you important.
He is in your corner when you're cornered.
He turns up when you get turned down.
All he wants in return for his helping hand is your hand shake. He never insists on seeing you except when nobody else wants to.
He raps your critics when they're wrong and takes the rap for you when they're right.
The only way he sponges off you is to absorb some of your troubles so you can have strength to fight the heel.
When you're taking bows, he bows out. You can do anything you want to with his friendship except buy it or sell it.
He makes you realize that having a real friend is like having an extra life. All he asks of your friendship is the privilege of deserving it.

Jeff used to tell me, "I know two great people in all the world" And I would just wait in eager anticipation for him to name me as the second one of them when he would say with a big smile, "And you're both of them!" Jeff was always such an encourager. I put him on a pedestal and kept him there. He was the best, believe me! If only you could have a "Jeff" in your life, you would be blessed!!!

Be Proactive and Productive

The way to get started is to quit talking and begin doing

Walt Disney

Don't just sit around! Go out there and push on some doors! Be proactive. Ask questions! Don't just wait for opportunities to come to you! We only have one chance at life, so don't mess it up. The clock is ticking. Work hard now! You are losing daylight.

Another mentor of mine, General Dick Abel, has always done this. His character is impeccable. He's in the same league as Billy Graham. He's been faithful to his wife and family to a tee! He is proactive and is a producer. He had three careers which included the Air Force, the Olympic Committee, and Christian Ministry. He held executive leadership positions in each of these careers. His is full of integrity and can been trusted without reservation.

He wasn't afraid to take on the tough issues. He was tough but fair, when he investigated the facts. He was an encourager. He helped me many times, and I can honestly say that had he not intervened, I probably would not have re-joined the Air Force after being unfairly dealt a severe injustice. He has always been in my corner even though he knows my flaws to a tee and jokes about them. He is in a wheelchair now and spending his last days on earth. I'll never forget something he told me when he was at the end of his formal Christian Ministry, "Billy, I want to sprint to the finish line!" There's a guy who won't give up.

Michael Jordan, one of the best basketball players of all time said, "Sometimes, things may not go your way, but the effort should be there every single night."

That's Dick Abel to a tee. But making money was never his goal. He fathered, he mentored, he taught, he counseled, he spoke publicly, and he wrote books. He was always being productive. Even from his wheelchair and just having had a stroke, he called people to check up on them, he spent time with God and he loved his wife and children. There are many crowns in heaven awaiting this precious saint. I hope to help him carry them around! With mixed emotions, I must tell you that Gen Abel passed away just prior to the publishing of this book.........

Self-Image

The most important determination to having a good self-image is obeying your conscience. God gave each one of us a conscience. We inherently know right from wrong, even at an early age. The Ten Commandments help us, but we don't have to have them to know it is wrong to steal or to kill someone.

While I'm on this subject, avoid anyone who is cruel to animals. If one of your friends thinks it's cool to hurt a little puppy or to kill a little kitten, flee from them right away! Something is really wrong with that person! They have a flawed conscience. And it's amazing to me how many criminals in prison who ended up killing people, who first started with mutilating animals! So sad to me......Run away from these people!!!

God created us in His image. We start out as a reflection of who He is. Only after sin enters our being and is not dealt with by repentance and forgiveness, do we deviate from His likeness. We all do things wrong as we travel on our life journey. But the trick is when you find yourself in the ditch, get out quickly. Listen to your conscience, confess what you have done wrong, receive forgiveness from God and others whom you might have offended and try not to make the same mistake again. If you do this, you will have a good self-image. That is God's desire for you, and you will be able to love others if you love yourself first. You have to be healthy to help those in need, which is also God's perfect will.

To have a healthy self-image, one of the doctors at the Cleveland Clinic has six suggestions:

> 1. *Remember what it was like to be a kid*
> 2. *Experience and express gratitude*
> 3. *Praise others liberally*
> 4. *Have a plan for self-growth and enact it with determination*
> 5. *Take social media breaks*
> 6. *Notice your sensitivities*

Don't believe THE Press or YOUR Press

> *Humility isn't denying your strengths; it's being honest about your weaknesses*
> *Rick Warren, famous Christian author*

In days past the press would report the news. Now they have a big-time agenda and slant the news according to what they want you to hear and believe. There are few journalists who do the hard work in order to really get to the bottom of a story and tell the facts from all angles. Today the press is focused on sensationalism and sales, not on reporting the facts in an unbiased manner. You can find the facts of a story, but most of the time you have to dig for them. Search for reliable reporting that is lightly biased.

And don't believe YOUR press if you become "important." Be realistic and down to earth in your self-evaluation. Some people fall in love with themselves after reading their press releases. This is the first step in their downfall!

Make Life Easy on Yourself

> *Don't squat on your spurs!*
> *Unknown Cowboy*

Don't do things that make life harder! Don't beat yourself up intentionally. The curve balls life throws at you will challenge you enough without putting yourself in the penalty box. Follow the advice of the people you admire and respect – specifically your parents and your mentors! Those are the ones who have made good choices over a long period of time.

Question them about why they made the decisions that they did. They will tell you the good, the bad and the ugly. No one makes right decisions all the time. We are flawed. But the happiest, most successful people are the ones that follow the rules, think critically and make good choices over a long period of time. It's never too late to turn things around.

We've all known people who are continually in trouble. Funny how some of the people in grade school who can't get it right, fail in high school, don't go to college or trade school, eventually end up in jail or prison. If you trace back their choices, you will find they lead to bad decisions. They beat themselves up instead of making life easy. Many times, these decisions involve drugs or alcohol.

Over your lifetime you will encounter many forks in the road, where you have to make a choice. It might be an important decision about who you run with, or it might be a decision about a difficult situation. Some decisions are pivotal and some are less impactful. As I said before, it's like the devil sitting on one shoulder and an angel sitting on the other shoulder. Here's an illustration I learned early in life from Dr James Dobson, the child psychologist, and I will never forget it, because the story is so powerful!

He told the story about two brothers whose father was an alcoholic. One of the boys did right, made good choices, had a meaningful life and was generally happy.

The other boy made a mess of his life. He drank a lot just like his father. He made poor choices, ended up in prison. Years later, a reporter doing a story on their lives, asked the same question. "How did you boys turn out so differently, given you both had the same alcoholic father?" Now read this carefully. They both had the same answer for the reporter. "With a father like mine, what would you expect?" Wow!!!

Will Rogers is a great humorous and is full of witty life lessons. Here's what he said on making financial decisions:

> *"Don't gamble; take all your savings and buy some good stock and hold it till it goes up, then sell it. If it don't go up, don't buy it."*

The bottom line is you can't predict the future, but you can plan for it.

Life Lesson #4 — Your Attitude

Weakness of attitude becomes weakness of character

Albert Einstein

Your attitude is one of the most important factors in how you conduct your life. Attitude determines altitude. You can choose to be optimistic and cheerful or go through life a dullard, always complaining, never achieving! When you do something over and over, consistently, it becomes a habit! Like pilots who have good habits when flying, develop good discipline in your developing your attitude!

Enjoy each day. It's a gift! In fact, the Apostle Paul in Ephesians, 5:20, reminds us, "And give thanks for everything to God the Father in the name of our Lord Jesus Christ."

I've heard so many stories of people who thought they would have another day and it never happened. No one is promised tomorrow. Don't become complacent about the 24 hours that God gives you each morning. Get outside, do something, even when the weather is bad. We are born with the ability to be winners or losers, but it's up to us to choose which one we will be. Nothing goes completely right for everyone, and nothing goes completely wrong for everyone. Develop the habit of being optimistic. See the glass as half full. Optimists are generally happy people.

Believe in miracles! They can happen! They do happen! They happen every day in every part of the world. Develop an attitude of gratitude! Be thankful for even the little things. King David in Psalms 100:1-5, gave us a great lesson about being thankful to God. It's a great message to memorize and meditate on......

Psalms 100

¹ Make a joyful noise unto the Lord,
*   all ye lands.*
² Serve the Lord with gladness:
*   come before his presence with singing.*
³ Know ye that the Lord he is God:
*   it is he that hath made us, and not we ourselves;*
*   we are his people, and the sheep of his pasture.*
⁴ Enter into his gates with thanksgiving,
*   and into his courts with praise:*
*   be thankful unto him, and bless his name.*
⁵ For the Lord is good;
*   his mercy is everlasting;*
*   and his truth endureth to all generations.*

You should always take the opportunity to express your gratitude to others who have helped or sacrificed for you. Generally speaking, I am a grateful person, and I've tried to express my gratitude for others in many ways. I am so thankful for my mother and the influence she had in my life. She affected my attitude toward life in a very meaningful way. One Christmas I felt moved to express this to her. I had it written in calligraphy and put into a nice frame. Here's what I wrote:

TO MY MOTHER

This Christmas present will be a little different from the normal ones you receive. Instead of the usual cardinal figurine, ocean picture, jewelry box, or electric kettle, I simply want to express my heartfelt appreciation to you for being my Mother.

Mum, I love you more than words can say. From my earliest memories of you listening to my tales of falling down and skinning my knee on the sidewalk in Alaska, and then cleaning the blood off with a cigarette filter, to trading my tricycle for a popsicle, you have been there to pick me up, dust me off, and give me wise advice. I have to tell you of my disappointment, though, when you came home from the hospital in Colorado and didn't have as many babies as our dog Cheena had puppies! Other than that, you've been perfect in every regard! As one little boy said, "You're the best Mother I've ever had"!

I admire your optimistic attitude, keeping yourself in shape, and your energetic approach to life. Despite a difficult first marriage, your courage, strength, and perseverance brought you and my sister and brothers through some hard times to a wonderful future. When you left Canada with four young children, no job, no home, and little money, you did what not one in a thousand women could do -- provided us a loving home, found a job, and within one year paid back a $1000 loan from Nanor. You've always had a bright outlook on life, no matter what your circumstances. That is a gift. For me this came into clear focus when you retired from the profession of teaching and library science. People came from all over to wish you well for being so faithful and having such a cheerful outlook every day. I believe in the years to come you will have many youngsters return and tell you what a profound influence you've had on their lives. You certainly have on mine. I am indebted to you. You have made a substantial contribution to the education of the youth of our nation. I wish you every blessing in life as you enjoy your retirement years. You've earned them.

People sometimes tell me that when I was born, they broke the mold, but I think the same could be said of you. After all, how many people are upset when a big snow fall misses their city? How many people want to "Dance with the baby with a hole in stockin'"" at the drop of a hat? Or how many people have watched Jay "Lenard" on TV, or read books at the "liberry", or "worshed" the dishes? In fact, you're the only one I know that greets all visitors "with bells on".

Even though some of our family traditions have seemed kind of silly, like playing "I Spy" on long trips, or wearing the Santa hat while opening Christmas presents, that sort of thing seemed to put cement in the building bricks of life. We practice those same silly traditions in my family today. And I am so thankful you gave me the freedom you did when I was in high school. I was fortunate we shared an honest relationship, where I could tell you exactly what I was doing and what was going on in my circle of friends. You weathered my formative years so well.

You know I loved your Mother, my favorite Grandmother, Nanor. So many of her superlative qualities have been passed on to you. I hope I have as many of your great traits as you have of hers. And even though I wrote a tribute to Nanor after she died, it's a shame she never got to read it on earth, the way you will be able to enjoy this one. Both of you have given me a real heart for God. Being a staunch Episcopalian, and so faithful to God, has given me a real foundation for my own faith, even as Nanor's love for God instilled a childlike faith in me. I've always admired your unswerving allegiance to Our Lord and Savior, Jesus Christ.

I remember when I graduated from high school. I didn't think it was a big deal until you gave me a very special present. Do you remember? You gave me a $100 bill! I was shocked, because I knew we were on a tight budget . You put it in a picture frame and presented it to me with love. I think you realized I would be leaving for the Academy and beginning life on my own. You had given me such confidence and sound principles to live by, I merely saw high school graduation as a transition in life. Throughout my Academy days you were so supportive. Every year I wanted to quit, you always encouraged me to stay, but left the final decision up to me. Today I'm glad I stayed. You have been equally supportive of my Air Force career.

I will never forget one visit to Kansas City, just in the last couple of years. I stayed for a few short days and was flying back to Dallas. I don't know if I ever told you, but it was so hard for me to walk down the walkway to the airplane for some reason that day. You said to me in your traditional fashion, "Now, is there anything I can do for you?" I thought, "My goodness, Mum, you've done so much already. How could you do more?" Then I got on the plane and cried and cried thinking about how much you loved me, and how much I loved you. A Mother's love just keeps on giving. Another time at the Academy I remember Stick and I staying up real late and talking about our childhood experiences. Before the night was over, we were bawling like a couple of kids, just reflecting on how much we adored our Mothers -- what unselfish love they always demonstrated to us through our lives. I freely admit that I'm a Momma's boy.

What can I say? There's much more of course. Much more. Yours is an unconditional, undying love demonstrated in the arena of life. You've done so much for me. You're an amazing person. I love you with a deep, life-long, appreciative, sincere love.

Your son, Bill

Winston Churchill said, "Attitude is a small thing that makes a big difference." And Thomas Jefferson once said, "Nothing can stop the man with the right mental attitude from achieving his goal; nothing on earth can help the man with the wrong mental attitude."

Can you see WHY attitude is so very important in the way we approach life? In your thinking, be a realist. In your communication with others, be an optimist!

Think Critically

> *The important thing is not to stop questioning. Curiosity has its own reason for existing.*
> Albert Einstein

This is a tough life lesson, because it's not taught in school. Have you ever heard of a critical thinking class being offered in high school or any university? Critical thinking is a forgotten art, and a dead science. You must think critically if you are going to come to the truth. Most people will not tell you the truth. Most people today would rather be caressed than told the truth. And with all the inputs you will have in life from family, friends, social media, and your own study, it will be your responsibility to separate the wheat from the chaff. If you discern the truth early, you will have a happier life!

Critical thinking is defined as the analysis of facts to form a judgment. The subject is complex with several different definitions. These include the rational, skeptical, and unbiased analysis or evaluation of factual evidence. Critical thinking is unconventional thinking. Critical thinking is thinking "outside the box." Develop into an independent, analytical thinker.

Thinking is harder than most folks imagine, which sounds like a tautology, but it's true! Pick a time and place to put in the effort.

There are eight principles of critical thinking:

1. Gather complete information.
2. Understand and define all terms.

3. Question the methods by which the facts are derived.
4. Question the conclusions.
5. Look for hidden assumptions and biases.
6. Question the source of facts.
7. Don't expect all of the answers.
8. Examine the big picture

Notice the steps sound like a systems engineering solution. The problem is our paradigm has shifted. People lie now all the time and suffer no consequences. A good friend of mine was remembering the "good ole days" when you would get caught lying in school and get a whipping for it. Then when you got home and your folks found out, you would get another whipping!

Not so today.... You lie in school, nothing happens because the schools really can't discipline, and if the school does call the parents, the parents blame the teacher or the administration for their child lying or stealing the answers or cheating on his test! And things are getting worse by re-writing history, teaching nonsense like "critical race theory", and setting the three R's aside in school.

I have a friend today that says when he deals with people, he just assumes they are lying! He says it makes it much easier to discern the truth! We have to question the information. The government is exceptionally bad about this. Coffee is good for you, and months later it is bad. Meat is a good source of protein, and then they want everyone to be vegan. We become energy independent, but then they incentivize everyone to electric vehicles, yet they have no plan for what to do with electricity shortages or worn-out batteries.

Who in the world knows about vaccines, boosters, masks and all the rest? You have to do your own research. You have to use the principles of critical thinking and then make up your own mind. Don't be controlled by the government, the TV, or social media. Think for yourself. Blaze through the lies and get to the truth. Consult as many sources as possible.

I am completely astounded that our country is so divided right now on every issue. No one is examining the facts. One reason for this is this fact is that the facts are hard to find! No one is using common sense, if there is any common sense left! How can intelligent people on both sides of the aisle disagree so vehemently, when they are both looking at the same facts! It astounds me! You have to get to the root cause of a problem to solve it.

One father, my classmate and roommate at The Air Force Academy, Jerry Cooke, taught his children to think critically at the dinner table. During their discussions someone would make a statement. He would always ask "Why"? They would explain and he would listen carefully. Then he would again ask, "Why"? After three or four iterations of this line of questioning, the children were really learning to think about what they said, and think why their statement would or would not stand up to scrutiny.

You've heard perception is reality. That's true. But everyone can't be driven by feeling. Examine the true facts and make a judgment. Do we have laws? We must follow them. Dr James Dobson pointed out a policeman shouting on a corner intersection all day long is not as effective as one ticket. Make a policy, and there are consequences. Give people free money and they won't go to work. It's not rocket science. Socialism breeds mediocrity. Be a skeptic. It will serve you well in life.

And even when you are young, tackle the tough issues. Choices have consequences. Elections have consequences. Give considerable thought to these questions:

Who am I? Why am I here? What is my greater purpose in life? What is truth? What is reality? Heavy stuff, but you will have a more meaningful life if you consider these questions early (late high school and college) in your life.

Critical thinking really comes down to renewing our mind and your perspectives. In Romans 12:2, we read: *"Do not conform any longer to the pattern of this world, but be transformed by the renewing of your mind. Then you will be able to test and approve what God's will is-- his good, pleasing and perfect will."*

All that sounds a little negative, and generally speaking I'm a glass half-full guy. I am very encouraged by home-school education and children raised in two-parent loving families that are slugging it out every day in the arena of life. Those kids are being taught the truth and they're being taught to think critically. They are fortunate, but they are also in the minority today. We need to make critical thinking a mandatory class in every school! It is substantially important!!

One of my life-time mentors, General Orwyn Sampson, taught me to be a critical thinker among many other things. He is a free thinker. He is an inventor. He has always welcomed new ideas and new thoughts throughout his long life. He is so secure in what he believes that new thoughts do not intimidate him. He entertains them with delight and examines them from every angle. He taught me biochemistry, microbiology, anatomy, and many other subjects in Pre-Med, and his approach and perspective were always unique. I owe him so much. He has always tried to keep me on track with his sound wisdom. Back in 2003, I wrote him a short note of thanks for his profound impact in my life:

General Sampson,

I would like to thank you for the profound influence you've had on my life. I could never repay you for the advice, counsel, and direction you've given me for over 30 years. You have truly been an inspiration to me by your words, actions, and witness. You've have never disappointed me, and you and Diane have always been there for the girls and me. My long association with you and your family has been a true blessing in my life. You have to have the most hospitable family in the whole world. We always feel so comfortable when we visit, and you have shared not only your lives, but your home with us many times over the years. You have set the benchmark of values for me. I look forward to our continued fellowship. I appreciate you taking the time to drive up from Colorado this weekend. It means a whole lot to me. You have been there supporting and guiding me my entire career. I couldn't have done it without your encouragement. You are my hero!

You have modeled the life of a Christian, a Father and a husband for me.........I didn't have to read about it in the Bible, because it was displayed in living color for me.

With the greatest respect and admiration,

Bill

Don't let emotion rule your life

> *Never make a permanent decision based on a temporary emotion*
>
> *Anonymous*

A nation is best served when governed as a republic with democratic principles and honest leaders who are Godly men. So too, your life will be much better off if you govern yourself not by emotion but by faith, character and logic.

When discussing faith, many Christians say in order to be a Christian you have to take a "leap of faith." This is NOT true. You do have to trust God, but it's not a leap. It's just cracking the door open a little. It's looking at nature around you and seeing the creative genius of God and then asking Him to be part of your life.....opening the door just a little and letting Him take over. It's still hard, but it's not some giant leap of faith.

Here's what the Apostle Paul says about trusting God in Ephesians 4: 17-19; *"Then Christ will make his home in your hearts as you trust in him. Your roots will grow down into God's love and keep you strong. And may you have the power to understand, as all God's people should, how wide, how long, how high, and how deep his love is. May you experience the love of Christ, though it is too great to understand fully. Then you will be made complete with all the fullness of life and power that comes from God."*

As sure as the sun sets and rises each day, as sure as gravity effects each walking step, the Lord is true and constant. His ways are proven and unchanging and His love is everlasting. Ask Him to prove that to you, and He will walk with you on your faith journey.

One of my closest favorite friends in life, a guy I roomed with at the Air Force Academy, is "Stick" or Mark Stickney, a military brat just like me who was raised in New Hampshire. He is the best friend you'll ever meet. A kind and gentle soul and a person of great integrity and a great sense of humor. I involved him in far too many of my pranks, but he did survive the Academy and went on to be a commercial airline pilot retiring eventually from Delta Airlines.

At night, Stick and I would have many discussions on religion. Both of us were raised in Protestant denominational households. He knew I was "religious", but that didn't bother him as he got to know me. I prayed for Stick from the minute we first roomed together to have a personal relationship with Jesus, explaining to him that being a Christian had little to do with religion, and everything to developing a relationship with the Creator of the Universe!

Being an engineer, he wanted to see the evidence and the facts. I told him they were there, but it also involved a step of faith including trusting God and relinquishing your life to Him. Along with that, to follow his direction in order to get to know Him better. The happy news is Stick became a Christian and told me something one night I'll never forget. He said, "You know, Bill, when you crack that door, it's like Jesus puts his foot inside so you can't shut it again!" Well, I don't know about that theology, but I did always admire Stick's sincerity. Of course, we are still life-long best friends today.

Recently he was asked to give a talk at his church about his faith. Here's what he said:

"Hi, I'm Mark Stickney. My wife Jayne and I have been members here at FBCH for about 3 years.

I grew up in a military family attending non-denominational Protestant churches, changing churches every two to three years when Dad changed assignments.

Looking back, there were two life-changing events I'd like to share.

First, in my senior year of high school, I became aware of Brian Piccolo, a 26-year-old running back for the Chicago Bears. He was a teammate and roommate with Gale Sayers. Incidentally, this was the first NFL interracial roommate arrangement. Gale Sayers was so inspired by Brian and his life that he wrote a book entitled "I Am Third" that ultimately inspired the made for television film "Brian's Song." The phrase, "I Am Third," became a lifelong inspiration for me. God, my Lord, is first. My family and friends are second. And finally, I am third.

Second, during my four-year residence at the Air Force Academy I met Bill Murray and eventually we became roommates. Bill was and is still today, my best male friend, confidant, and role model. I credit him for my true "spiritual awakening", through Bible studies, conversations, and the many adventures we shared all through the years. He is the person you see in the crowd that exudes that "Christian Glow" and "Eye Twinkle". It reminds me of Matthew 5:14-16 which states:

"You are the light of the world. A city situated on a hill cannot be hidden. No one lights a lamp and puts it under a basket, but rather on a lampstand, and it gives light for all who are in the house. In the same way, let your light shine before men, so that they may see your good works and give glory to your Father in Heaven."

After 46 years of work and travels, Jayne and I decided to settle and retire in Western NC. How fortunate we both feel to have found a solid God loving Bible teaching church like First Baptist to nurture and feed us on our spiritual journey.

Character is developed over time. Character is a summation of your deposits of good choices over a life time. When you look at someone and think he has good character or bad character, what do you include in the parameters?

Integrity has to be first. Are you truthful, sincere, and trustworthy? Secondly, are you kind, thoughtful, mannerly, and consider others' needs before your own? Do you treat your neighbor like you would like to be treated?

Now we come to logic. And here's a bit of controversial logic. I'm going out on a limb to say that men generally tend to think more from a basis of logic and women tend to think more from a basis of feeling. This can be proven, but it certainly not accepted today in our politically correct society. And I will say there are benefits to both, but being governed feelings will not get you where you want to go. Fortunately for me, my wife thinks both ways, but most of the time I can have logical discussions with her. For some of my married friends, that is not the case with their wives, which makes things difficult sometimes. God Bless them......... Even if you both don't think the same way, you try to understand the other person's perspective, which supports a healthy relationship in all cases and in all communication!

Let your life be governed by logic. Think critically. If the true data doesn't support the conclusion, no matter how you feel about it, then don't go there. Logic is closely tied to common sense, and common sense is closely tied to gut instinct or conscience. Just identify emotional responses and filter most of them out. If it looks like a duck and talks like a duck, then it probably is a duck.

One of the places young people run into major problems is when they think "they're in love"... And many times, they are! I've been in love many times! But most of the time I was in love with being in the "moment of being infatuated"! Yet, to find your true soul mate in life, your decisions can't be based upon "feeling in love" exclusively. Do not rely or count on warm fuzzies! Choose to love someone because you can't live without them, they fulfill you and make you a better person, they complete you and want to walk in unison with your mutual vison of life on earth and after life.

Choose someone to love for a lifetime because they have the character you want to see in your spouse, not because they look like a model or a movie star. Those looks will fade with time. It's called old age and no one has found the fountain of youth yet! Of course, doing the right thing is hard to do, if you believe you're in love.

I suggest relying on the advice of your parents (if they have good character and live their lives according to solid principles), the principles of scripture, and the unbiased opinion of your mentors. Most of the time doing those three things will keep you out of trouble, no matter how strong the love pull is. And it is strong. God designed it that way! Don't fight it……enjoy it, but make your important decisions in life based on logic, not feelings!

People remember how you made them feel

> *Unless someone like you cares a whole awful lot*
> *Nothing's going to get better.*
> *No, it's not.*
>
> *–Dr. Seuss*

People will not remember what you told them, but they will remember how you made them feel. Guard your tongue. Boy, is this true in spades! Remember your words are powerful. Think before you speak. You can crush someone's spirit in a second that takes a life-time to repair! In fact, sometimes you will never recover from an off-hand remark made in the simplest setting!

You may be the only book someone reads. If you don't have something good to say, then stay quiet. Spend at least two-thirds of your time listening. God gave you one mouth and two ears. Don't interrupt others. Don't be thinking about what you want to say when the other person is talking like I often do! Really listen! Don't ever miss the opportunity to shut up!

Slow down, speak carefully, and value others more than yourself. People have hurt me with their words, and I have hurt others I care most about, including my wife,

Judy, and our daughters, Rosemary and Evelyn. I hope they have forgiven me. Always remember that other people are important.

When Judy and I were a young couple in ministry, another Christian couple told us that we had too many non-Christian friends, that we were not worthy of their time to disciple, and that we would not make it as Christians in the long run. We were devastated. Both of us were strong in our faith, but this set us on our heels! I remember listening to a reel-to-reel player of a recording of a song that just said over and over again "I love you, I love you, I love you!" We listened to it all afternoon. That was 44 years ago. I'm sure this couple meant well, but had Judy and I not been such strong people, this could have sunk the ship!

Before I leave this topic, here are several more quotes to think about.

The greatest healing therapy is friendship and love
Hubert Humphrey

Don't count the days, make the days count
Muhammad Ali

Preach the gospel at all times, and when necessary, use words
Attributed to Saint Francis of Assisi, that great Saint

Don't be a complainer

This will be short.... Don't whine about things! No one likes a whiner. God does not like a whiner! Don't let circumstances rule the day! Train yourself to have a good attitude. Did you know it takes fewer muscles to smile than frown?

Adversity

As Joyce Meyer, Christian author, once said, *"Complaining is dangerous business. It can damage or even destroy your relationship with God, your relationships with other people, and even with your relationship with yourself."*

> *I can't change the direction of the wind, but I can adjust my sails to always reach my destination*
> *Jimmy Dean, sausage maker*

> *Obstacles are those frightful things you see when you take your eyes off your goal*
> *Henry Ford, maker of the first automobile*

> *Start by doing what's necessary; then do what's possible; and suddenly you are doing the impossible.*
> *Saint Francis of Assisi*

It's a fact that in this life, you **WILL** have adversity. Expect challenges and don't be surprised when you fail. This is part of the learning process. This is one of the ways you become smarter, learn to love more deeply, and find ways to build a stronger character. I love the saying, "Better to have loved than never to have loved at all." That quote is from Lord Alfred Tennyson who wrote that in a poem in honor of a friend who recently died. It has been so true for me.

The key to understanding adversity is knowing it will come and come again throughout your life. And successfully dealing with adversity depends largely upon your attitude. Your attitude when dealing with adversity is the single key that will make a difference in your life and the lives around you. Whether you are leading or following, make it a priority to have a great attitude. As a man thinks, so is he. Leaders are good at facing adversity. They anticipate it, deal with it, and move on.

They view adversity as an opportunity, not as a road block!

If you are a Christian, you have the advantage in dealing with adversity, because Jesus is on your side. It's even better when you let Him take the wheel! (Remember the song by Carrie Underwood) God is watching after you, like your best friend, and will make all things new and right in His time. And keep in mind, your timetable for defeating or overcoming adversity is probably much shorter than His for the reasons stated in the first paragraph in this section!

Sometimes adversity will come in the form of testing your faith. When your faith is tested, your endurance has a chance to grow. In fact, when you face adversity of any kind, you will have to be patient. And when your endurance is mature, you will be a much better person of character. Little will be able to rock your boat. You can't tell how good a man or a watermelon is until they get thumped!

No one lives on the mountain top all the time. In fact, when you're on the mountain top, there is only one direction to go, and it's not up! Life is a series of hills and valleys. Celebrate the good times, but don't fear the bad. God will never give you more than you can handle. His grace is sufficient for your every trial. This is true, but hard to believe given the circumstances of some people's lives! Don't fear adversity, even though you know it is coming. Welcome it as a tool to improve your relationship with God and your developing character.

When you face adversity, take some time to retreat. Get alone. Analyze the situation. Ask God for help. Ask others more mature than you for advice. Don't count on others facing the trial for you, and when you make your decision on how you will handle the adversity, don't blame others. Force yourself to think about options and solutions. Pray, trust God, and go to work on solving the problem. Life comes in phases; some are great times and others not so great. No one likes adversity, but it will come. Train yourself to be courageous! When you get knocked down or you fail miserably, you must get back up, put your face to the wind, and start again by putting one foot ahead of the other, one step at a time. You are developing patient endurance through the process.

Turn fatigue into fortitude. You must learn how to conquer the temptation in order to stop the sin. Success is when you want to quit, but you don't. It's an uphill battle, but your mind and body are stronger than you think they are. Few people are brought to their limits mentally or physically in life. My experiences at the Air Force Academy in academics, sports, and survival training came close, but I always had some reserve. You can do more than your mind will let you believe. Seal training is a great example of this principle.

I love this......

> *"Promise me you'll always remember:*
> *you're braver than you believe,*
> *stronger than you seem,*
> *and smarter than you think."*

Winnie-the-Pooh

Finally, I leave you with one last positive thought on this tough process. In this life and the next, the final answer has been decided. The war has been won, if you have given yourself totally to the Lord. He is the ultimate overcomer. He conquered death, and He alone can give you life eternal with Him forever.

You will overcome in the end.

Be Kind

Kindness is a language which the deaf can hear and the blind can see
                                                    Mark Twain

In life, you'll catch more bees with honey. That's what my daughter Rosemary always says, and she should know, because there's no one nicer in the world than her! Mercy triumphs over judgement. Kindness works over harshness. Be known as a kind person. Don't be critical and harsh. Jesus said, "Let the little children come unto me."

When I was at the Air Force Academy, it seemed like I was always getting into trouble. I was so rebellious that I was often restricted to campus. However, I could visit the Chaplain, Col Johnson, and his wife, Mrs. Johnson. Mrs. Johnson was always so nice to me. She would listen carefully to my woes and how harsh the Upper Classmen had been to me for no good reason. She was so kind, empathetic, and motherly. I loved to be in her company. She would always laugh at my jokes and took my side in every situation.

Marlene Dietrich, an actress from early Hollywood, once said, *"Kind words can be short and easy to speak their echoes are truly endless"*. That's absolutely true because, even though I'm 70, I remember those days and Mrs Johnson's kindness like it was yesterday. I loved Mrs. Johnson and I still do. We still laugh about things and share our lives together today. It's quite possible her kindness kept me at the Air Force Academy when all I wanted to do was quit and go home.

Smile

A smile makes everyone look immeasurably more attractive. Smiles, like hugs are contagious. As I said, it takes more muscles to frown than it does to smile. That means it is easier to smile. Do you know what the difference is between sad and happy people? If you take a good look, happy people have pleasant wrinkles.

<u>Trials</u>

Optimism is the faith that leads to achievement. Nothing can be done without hope and confidence
–Helen Keller, the little girl born deaf and blind

Life is not easy or fair and life can be tough at times. Just ask Helen Keller, who because of a childhood illness was deaf and blind since infancy. But as I've always told my girls, hang in there. Things change. Do the right thing and keep doing it. Circumstances change. What seems like a mountain that can't be moved, one day will be gone in a week or a month or a year. Have hope! Be optimistic. See the glass as half full, not half empty. Don't be a Debbie Downer. That's easy! Helen Keller had hope, and lived a long and successful life.

Take an eternal view of your circumstances. The rain falls on the good and the bad. Bad things happen to good people. Sometimes because of their bad choices, but not all the time. Sometimes they happen out of an innocent decision or minor mistake, or sometimes they just happen for no reason.

What is vital is how you respond! Is it "Woe is me" for the rest of your life, or do you get up when you're knocked down? The answer is you get up because you know you have a purpose in life, that you a special, that you are in the process of change, and that you have a vision and a hope beyond this world? God will always be beside you! He will never leave you! He will never let anything come into your life that you can't handle or that He will not give you the strength or grace to overcome.

When the Apostle Paul prays for the Christians at the Church in Colossae, he writes in 1:9-10, "So we have not stopped praying for you since we first heard about you. We ask God to give you complete knowledge of his will and to give you spiritual wisdom and understanding. Then the way you live will always honor and please the Lord, and your lives will produce every kind of good fruit. All the while, you will grow as you learn to know God better and better."

We are all on a spiritual journey of seeking, learning, understanding and honoring God by producing good fruit. And when you grow, you will get to know Jesus better. He will lead you.

I love the poem *"Footsteps in the Sand,"* that tells of a person walking along the beach with Jesus. All of the sudden where there were two sets of footprints, there became only one. The person walking beside Jesus said, "You left me when my trial was the greatest"! But the punch line of the poem says "No, when your trial was the greatest, that's when I carried you!" What a fantastic poem! What a fantastic and true message. God will not give you anything in your life that you both can't handle, even though sometimes you challenge will seem insurmountable! Hang in there and have hope. Things will change, and most of the time they change for the better!

In life we will have trials. God allows them. Sometimes He brings them. We don't know what the thoughts of God are, but here are four reasons He may allow trials to come to you:

    1. To teach us that we reap what we sow.
    2. To develop our character to be more like His character
    3. To have empathy for others going through *trials*

> 4. To put us in situations where only He could provide the solution and not us. To make it abundantly clear He is the life giver

Many times, the fourth reason happens in hospitals. You are on your death bed. The doctors have done all they can do. Your parents and friends have offered all the prayers they can. Everyone has cried all they can and there seems to be no hope. Then all of the sudden, for no apparent reason, you live! God saved you in order to teach you that He alone is the Life Giver, here on earth and for eternity. And that is a long time...

I mentioned Dave Young earlier. He is my great close friend and life-time mentor. Dave is a real encourager. At one point in my life, I was really low. I was 59 years old and I had just been let go from my job at Lockheed Martin. I had prostate cancer, and I had just finished radiation treatments. I thought, "I don't know where to go or where to turn. I know God loves me, but all the options I see in front of me are not as good as working for Lockheed Martin. My boss, a military man, had just left me on the battlefield and I was bleeding to death. I would have to trust God, but this would be a hard thing for me to do at this point in my life; a very hard thing!

Dave sent me this note to remind me of what I already knew, but it came exactly at the right time...God's time... and I have read it many, many times since. And you know the rest of the story. Being let go from Lockheed Martin was one of the very BEST things that has ever happened to me! It led to me being hired by American Airlines for a whole new career with flying benefits, short work hours, and doing something that I love to do; teaching pilots! Here's what Dave sent me:

I know the plans I have for Bill Murray, declares the Lord ... Plans not for calamity, but for great gain. And I the Lord will bring it about in My time. Do not fear for I am with you, Bill, do not anxiously look about you for I am your God. I will strengthen you. I will help you. Surely, I will uphold you with My Righteous and powerful right hand. Set your eyes and heart on Me. I lift up nations and companies like Lockheed and I put them down. These are nothing to Me. I give my servants jobs for a season and take them away. These are nothing to Me and do not define the value of My children. My eyes are roaming over the face of the earth for men who are focused on Me. Men who are not entangled by the affairs of the world. Men who are not distracted by the worries of the world. When I find them, I will strongly support them. I will thwart their enemies. Be strong and courageous. Fight the good fight of Faith. Take hold of the Eternal Life to which you were called. And lo I am with you always, even to the end of the age, and surely through this new adventure that I have called you to. Do not say there are four months and then comes the gain. Lift up your eyes and see that the harvest is already ripe. I have not forsaken you. I have appointed the exact times and places for you to live. Do not worry about what you will wear nor what you will eat nor where you will live. Consider the sparrow sold for 2 cents. He does not toil yet does not worry about these things for I provide. Surely you, for whom I sent my Son and for whom His blood was shed, has no concern. I did not spare My own Son. I will freely give you all these things, exceeding, abundantly above your ability to ask or even imagine.

The following paragraph is what I emailed back to Dave. Notice that I'm trying to follow what I know is right, not let my feelings get in the way, trying to rely on God and His faithfulness, but I have to admit I was a little shaky and a little unbelieving, just like the Jews in the Wilderness, even though God had proven Himself to them over and over again. I knew circumstances would change, but I couldn't imagine how they could change for the better. I'm ashamed now that I was not more believing and trusting and solid. But, if I am transparent, I was hurting.

Thanks, Dave...I leave for 5 days in the morning to go visit Paul in Oregon. I've been a little down due to all of this...realizing that God is in control and would have to do this to force me to change directions. You can drive yourself crazy thinking how you could have done things differently, or how in the world the Human Resources Dept could have judged your record and performance the way they did. You just have to believe, obey and not let your feelings rule...tough to do sometimes when you don't want to go out this way, rather on your own terms. One thing I know from life is circumstances change...you have to be patient and trust the Author.

The Bible is filled with verses about hope. Here are a few of my favorite ones:

- *"But those who hope in the Lord will renew their strength. They will soar on wings like eagles; they will run and not grow weary; they will walk and not be faint." Isaiah 40:31*
- *"Let us hold unswervingly to the hope we profess, for he who promised is faithful." Hebrews 10:23*
- *"Now I know in part; then I shall know fully, even as I am fully known. And now these three remain: faith, hope, and love; but the greatest of these is love." 1 Corinthians 13:13*
- *"As for me, I will always have hope; I will praise you more and more." Psalm 71:14*
- *"And hope does not put us to shame, because God's love has been poured out into our hearts through the Holy Spirit, who has been given to us." Romans 5:5*

Because we serve a God of hope, my prayer for you is the same as the Apostle Paul wrote to the church at Rome in Romans 15:13 *"I pray that God, the source of hope, will fill you completely with joy and peace because you trust in him. Then you will overflow with confident hope through the power of the Holy Spirit."*

> *Learn from yesterday, live for today, hope for tomorrow. The important thing is not to stop questioning.*
>
> *Albert Einstein*
>
> *Psalms Chapter 71:14 Verse 14 "As for me, I will always have hope; I will praise you more and more.*
>
> *King David*

Finances and Learning to be Content

> *It isn't what you have or who you are or where you are or what you are doing that makes you happy or unhappy. It is what you think about it.*
> *Dale Carnegie, author and philanthropist*

Live within your means. Spend less than you make. **Live at a little lower standard than you can afford.** Don't always be pushing the limits of your spending. It will only bring you stress and grief. Money will never make you happy!

I once led a guy to the Lord. He is one I mentioned earlier....one of my closest friends in the world. His name is Dave Young. Right now, I sit at his feet, because he has passed me by so quickly in knowledge, wisdom, and right living. I could write an entire chapter about Dave and our relationship, but suffice it to say, he's one of my best friends in life. He is loving, kind, giving, a straight talker, and a critical thinker. He accepts nothing at face value. He mulls it over and comes to his own decisions, which are 99% of the time right on the money.

When we get together he never fails to thank me for introducing him to Jesus, helping him get started, and walking alongside him. When he started his faith journey, he shortly rocketed by what I had to offer him growing in the Navigator ministry and choosing godly mentors.

However, I did offer him some financial advice in his early Christian life, that he has faithfully followed, and that has given him and his family great dividends. I told him early on to save 10% of his money, give 10% of his money to God, and do what he wanted with the rest. He has been very disciplined in doing that, and all his needs are met today, despite earning a very low salary for many years while in Germany on staff with the Navigators. God blessed him, because he honored God.

Most people don't have the financial discipline that Dave and his wife, Sally, do, but as a result of his saving discipline, he is a big-time giver to God and others now. Dave's charity gives him much pleasure. He lives within his means, doesn't try to keep up with the Jones, and makes wise decisions with the funds God has entrusted him to manage.

Dave employs the same principles of managing money to most other areas of his life, and this has made him very successful in life. Not just financially, but with his relationships with his friends, wife, family and farm. He is happy. He has mentored many people, including me, and invests his life in people to make a positive difference in their lives. He is a role model. And I'm proud to say he's my friend. And as Mark Twain wrote, *"Good friends, good books, and a sleepy conscience: this is the ideal life."*

In pilot training, they used to tell student pilots to save the $100 per month that we got for flight pay, because your non-flying contemporaries were not getting that bonus. If you did that, at the end of your career, if you invested that money conservatively, you would have saved over $100,000! Great advice, but I only know of one pilot who ever followed it.

Pay off your credit cards every month. Do not pay a penny of interest to the banks! Don't get yourself in debt, except for a home. Save for retirement. Don't compare yourself to others. That only causes you to covet. All that glitters is not gold. Dr James Dobson once said, *"The grass may be greener on the other side, but it still has to be mowed."*

Dr James Dobson also said, *"The more you own, the more that owns you"*! He was so right! Ray Leach, my lifetime F-111 friend who is 14 years my senior, and I play golf on a really nice country club. As we make our way down the first fairway, we often comment about the million-dollar-plus homes on either side of the fairway. We both could afford to pay a mortgage on one of those homes with five bedrooms, four car garages, swim pool, verandas, and multi-angled roofs. But, we also are quick to say, "even if we were given a home like those, we wouldn't take it!"

We don't want to clean them, pay the taxes on them, do the upkeep on them, or get lost in them trying to find our wives! Don't get me wrong....we both live in nice homes, but we live below our means. We spend less than we make, and we're both savers, and our wives help us and support us in our financial strategy.

Doing that has provided us a cushion in retirement to finish out our lives here on earth and help others. Some people call us cheap. I call us frugal. We have enough put back for a rainy day. And we are content with what we have. We both drive used cars and love dogs. We enjoy the simple things in life. We are not tempted by material things. Our struggles are in other areas.

One of the main causes of big problems in marriage is money. The more quickly you get on the same page with your spouse (hopefully in pre-marital counseling before you make a life-long covenant), the faster you can eliminate that problem. Have a common vision for your finances. Have the same strategy for your money and be disciplined about the way you handle money.

As I said before, life is not fair! Life will never be fair. It's never been fair, and how you define fair also makes a difference on how you see how fair life is! The sooner you learn this principle about being content, the happier you'll be. Don't expect life to be fair. Sometimes you'll get a better deal, and sometimes you'll get a crummy deal. Your attitude makes all the difference. On balance things will level out if you follow the life lessons in this book. If you don't, you get the results you get by your poor choices. Life is not easy. Learn to be content.

And also know this. God says, to the people of Israel and also to us, in the Book of Jeremiah, 31:3, "Long ago the LORD said to Israel: I have loved you, my people, with an everlasting love. With unfailing love I have drawn you to myself."

Henry Wadsworth Longfellow, poet and philosopher wrote, *"For after all, the best thing one can do when it is raining is let it rain."* In the midst of trials, God is there with us and pulling for us and cheering us on, wanting us to be content with what He has provided! Don't forget. He owns it all.

Humility

> *You're so vain, you probably think this song is about you*
>
> *Carly Simon, famous pop singer*

Humility is that one characteristic that you lose once you realize you have it. Don't be arrogant. Know your own personality. Some people are naturally egotistic. Others think that they can never measure up.

When I was in high school, a girl, Merilee Bealmare, used to tease me using the line from the Carly Simon song "You're so vain". I didn't even know what the word vain meant. But I've always had a great self-image, because my mother always believed in me. My mentors encouraged me. My family loved me. My friends thought the best about me.

But in your heart of hearts, if you think you're better than other people, you're in for some hard life lessons. If you think you're special and the rules don't apply to you, you're in for some hard lessons. There are few short cuts in life. Be humble. Don't think of yourself as being better than others. Everyone has different gifts and wonderful things they can offer to their families and communities. Be patient. Short cuts in life are wrong, just like they are in a race. Don't be tempted to take them! I have done this to my dismay......

Be humble and smart enough to avoid the pain of some of life's most difficult lessons brought on by your own stupidity. One of my mother figures I love so much, Mrs. Ann Abel, with of my lifetime mentor, General Abel, once told me, "Billy, DBD!" That means "Don't be dumb". I needed that reminder and I often need that reminder. Sometimes I get ahead of myself. The Lord loves those who are poor in spirit and come to Him with humble hearts. Avoid humiliation by being humble and having an accurate view of yourself. *Mother Teresa wrote in "The Joy in Loving: A Guide to Daily Living" there are a few ways we can practice humility:*

> *To speak as little as possible of one's self.*
> *To mind one's own business.*

Not to want to manage other people's affairs.
To avoid curiosity.
To accept contradictions and correction cheerfully.
To pass over the mistakes of others.
To accept insults and injuries.
To accept being slighted, forgotten and disliked.
To be kind and gentle even under provocation.
Never to stand on one's dignity.
To choose always the hardest.

Don't Be Afraid

We can easily forgive a child who is afraid of the dark; the real tragedy of life is when men are afraid of the light

Plato

Fear is an unusual phenomenon. It can motivate you or cripple you. Fear can paralyze you! But a little fear can help you study a little harder so you can pass that test. Fear can help you perform better in certain situations. But in general, don't be afraid. If you are a Christian, God has your best interest at heart. He wants you to live life and live it abundantly. He has your back.

Don't fear failure! The fear of failure is what stands between you and greatness. Failure is a great teacher and motivator. **Almost all successful people have experienced significant failure at some time in their careers.** What you learn in the midst of those failures can propel you to great success. Nothing is wrong with trying and failing. Take a risk. What is wrong is not trying or not trying hard enough. Failure is in the path of every successful person, because they took a risk. And what's more is most of the things we fear never come about anyway! As John Lennon, one of two lead writers for the Beatles band wrote:

"There are two basic motivating forces: fear and love. When we are afraid, we pull back from life. When we are in love, we open to all that life has to offer with passion, excitement, and acceptance. We need to learn to love ourselves first, in all our glory and our imperfections. If we cannot love ourselves, we cannot fully open to our ability to love others or our potential to create. Evolution and all hopes for a better world rest in the fearlessness and open-hearted vision of people who embrace life."

When confronted by an uncertain situation, you will have to make a fight or flight decision. But if you are experiencing extreme fear, sometimes you may find yourself incapable of making a decision.

As Shakespeare wrote, *"Extreme fear can neither fight nor fly."*

> *He who has overcome his fears will be truly free.*
> *Aristotle*

Anger

> *Don't let the sun go down while you are still angry, for anger gives a foothold to the devil*
> *The Apostle Paul*

Don't be an angry person. Be thankful in all things. You can't be thankful and angry at the same time. Ecclesiastes 7:9 tells us, *"Anger resides in the bosom of fools."* Be a forgiving person. When you're angry, it hurts only you. Anger can eat you alive. And often times the person you are angry with has forgotten about the situation, and you, and moved on!

Anger is the opposite of God's nature. In Psalms 103:8, 13-18, King David writes, "The LORD is compassionate and merciful, slow to get angry and filled with unfailing love. The LORD is like a father to his children, tender and compassionate to those who fear him. But the love of the LORD remains forever with those who fear him. His salvation extends to the children's children of those who are faithful to his covenant, of those who obey his commandments!"

The Bible says to forgive others and you will be forgiven. The opposite is also true. If you don't forgive others, you will not be forgiven. Be a forgiving person. Sometimes this seems like an impossible task. Take for instance the drunk driver who hits and kills your child. How could you ever forgive that person? It's almost impossible to do so, but if you can't find that path of forgiveness, hate and anger will eat you up. It will shorten your life and make you forever miserable. God will give you the grace to forgive any transgression taken against you.

For married couples a good general rule of thumb is "Don't let the sunset fall on your anger." In other words, a good general rule is to ask for forgiveness from your mate before you go to bed. Now, I will allow an exception to this. If you are just too tired to work things out, and you're just going around the mountain for the hundredth time, and you have a spouse who likes to argue or always have the last word, then I suggest you call a truce, ask for forgiveness and work out the details after a good night's sleep.

Having positive relationships is healthy for the brain and the heart. Satisfying interactions stimulate the brain and causes neural circuits in the middle of the prefrontal cortex. In addition, positive "give and take" helps to regulate our emotions and gives us perseverance, which is also good. It helps us control negative impulses and aids in self-control, all of which I have written about in relationship to good character. Humans are wired to be in relationships with each other and with God. Keep those relationships open and honest giving no place for anger to gain root.

An angry person has serious problems. You should try to avoid angry people. Don't be close friends with an angry person. Certainly, don't choose a mentor or mate who is an angry person!

In line with Apostle Paul, in his quote at the beginning of this section, we don't want to give the devil any part of our lives, our time, our thoughts, or our actions! *In Psalms 104:34, King David reminds us, "May all my thoughts be pleasing to him, for I rejoice in the LORD."*

Furthermore, in one of my favorite verses, the Apostle Paul in Philippians 4:8 writes about the specific things we should let enter our minds: *"Finally, brothers and sisters, whatever is true, whatever is noble, whatever is right, whatever is pure, whatever is lovely, whatever is admirable—if anything is excellent or praiseworthy—think about such things."*

This would be an excellent verse to commit to memory.

Life Lesson #5 — Entering into Maturity

Pursue Genuine Manhood

An acorn is not an oak when it is sprouted. It must go through long summers and fierce winters, and endure all that frost, and snow, and thunder, and storms, and side-striking winds can bring, before it is a full-grown oak. So a man is not a man when he is created; he is only begun. His manhood must come with years. He who goes through life prosperous, and comes to his grave without a wrinkle, is not half a man. Difficulties are God's errands and trainers, and only through them can one come to the fullness of manhood.
Henry Ward Beecher

We need the iron qualities that go with true manhood. We need the positive virtues of resolution, of courage, of indomitable will, of power to do without shrinking the rough work that must always be done.
Theodore Roosevelt

What is being a man? What is genuine manhood? Our social media would have you believe that being a man is being macho, in great shape, handsome, with magnificent hair blowing in wind, driving a Tesla or Porsche, having a fat bank account, and having a great looking blonde in the other seat of your convertible. That's not even close!

Being a man means understanding and fulfilling your identity, your God-given purpose, fulfilling your responsibilities through faith, humility, gratitude, courage and perseverance. That's what true manhood is about!

Genuine manhood represents staying power in the face of adversity and the discipline to persist rather than give up, quit, or cut and run when things get tough!

Be a tender warrior: Pursue wisdom.....competence in your God-given skill set and slowly develop confidence with others who will encourage you in the race of life. If you are committed to the Lordship of Jesus Christ, you will be on the right track and you will be in submission to His will, and you will be happy and fulfilled in your life! Don't be selfish. Serve other people. Help other people. Be a giver and not a taker. That is what manhood is about. First please the Father, then look to others. A godly man is a genuine man, and he will persist in his relentless pursuit of Jesus all the way on his faith journey through the wilderness, through the valley of the shadow of death, and on the mountain top experiences of life.

Some advice for Parents

> *The one thing your child will not forgive you for is if you do not discipline them*
> Dr. James Dobson

As I wrote in the first section of this book, teach your children how to have a relationship with Jesus. Teach them obedience by the way you obey the Father. Teach your children to work hard, because we reap what we sow. Give your children some good memories! Your children only have one chance at growing up. Make it a positive experience for them. Take them on trips. Get them involved in sports and crafts.

Help them to discover their innate gifts and skills. Show them that there is a world outside the family and a big world outside of their city. If you don't have money to travel abroad, take them to the library. Have them join clubs after school, but monitor what is going on and what is taught no matter what activity they are involved in. It's sad, but there is way too much evil in the world these days to turn them loose for very long in any setting with another adult or their peers.

Regarding discipline, our girls didn't have to worry about that. They told us that they thought they were being raised by Dr. Dobson and his book "Dare to Discipline", which I would highly recommend by the way!

Get yourself involved in a peer group, preferably a group Bible Study or Home Group, where you can bounce ideas off other parents and see what challenges they are facing. You are not in this alone. If your parents are living and they are of good character, make sure your children spend time with their grandparents. They can have a very positive influence on your children.

I will never forget the positive influence my maternal grandmother, Nanor, had on me. When my dad left the family, my mom was sure to take us to Nanor and Newt's (Nanor's husband) home on a regular basis. They were always so good to us. They loved us unconditionally! They only wanted the best for us. I was so sad when Nanor went to heaven. Here are some of my recorded memories of her from my book "Renegade Colonel":

Nanor had a deep faith in God and she was a giver. We would always go out to eat at a real restaurant when we were there in Springfield – normally at their favorite Chinese restaurant where all the staff knew her and Newt. She would proudly introduce each one of her grandchildren. We could order whatever we wanted at the restaurant, including a drink of our choice. That was a real treat for us. Mom would always try to curtail us, but Nanor would say, "Pat, let them order what they want. I want them to be happy and full when they leave."

Running a family

You will never be successful in life if you are not successful in your home. The principles you use in running a business are similar for running a home. Love never fails. Learn how to say "I'm sorry". Be humble and set arrogance aside. Learn how to find self-esteem at home. Many men and women can find success and self-esteem at work, but that is not true success. Only your family will be there when the music stops. Guard them, teach them, train the children and launch them into the world.

Teach them the principles of life in the home. Model the characteristics of Christ in what you do in the home. Remember their first concept of God comes from the father in the family. Teach your children to love, to think critically, to follow the commandments, to learn how to make friends, to learn how to make right choices, and to learn how to invest and handle money. Teach them to share and have a heart for the poor and downtrodden. Help them to have a heart for widows and help those in need. Teach them how not to be taken advantage of in their goodness. Teach them to be humble and not arrogant. Teach them to be respectful of others. Teach them to live quiet, impactful lives enjoying all the blessings God brings their way.

There wasn't anything Nanor wouldn't do for us. She loved us thoroughly and completely and it showed. When I was 16 years old, she let me drive their new Buick over to Silver Dollar City with my brothers and sister. What a thrill to drive a new car with air conditioning that ran well and had some power. Many people have wonderful grandmothers, but they wouldn't hold a candle to my grandmother. I loved her with all my heart.

As she and Newt got older, they couldn't hear very well. So, after all the children were put to bed, I could hear

Nanor and Newt in the living room re-living each and every event of the day recalling their favorite memories. She would call him "Shugee" – her term of endearment. She would say, "Shugee, do you think the children liked their toys this time? Do you think they got enough to eat? What do you think they would enjoy doing tomorrow?" She was always thinking about others.

Launch Your children

> *You've got to learn to let go and let your children fall, and fail. If you try to protect them from hurt, and always rush to their side with Band-Aids, they won't learn about life, and what is true, what works, what helps, and what are real consequences of certain kinds of behavior. When they do get hurt, which they will, they won't know how to take care of their grown selves. They won't even know where the aspirin is kept.*
>
> *Anne Lamott, author*

You want your children to love you, respect you, look to you for advice, and depend upon you when they are growing up. But there comes a time when they must transition to being young adults. That's when you want them to be independent. You might feel it's time to cut the lifeline, but that lifeline will never be completely cut. Once a parent, always a parent. There's still plenty of work ahead of you.

I learned this principle from Mike Mrasek, my neighbor and close friend. Talk to your children about the concept of "launching". Tell them that what you do in the home in their formative years is really preparation for when they become independent and young adults. That time is different for different children, but a good goal is 18 years of age for them to launch. That is a time when they should own their own car, make most of their own decisions, be in some kind of career training, and start to think about being financially independent and on their own.

If you talk about this concept as they are growing up, then it won't be a surprise to them when they reach the launching age. It won't be as if you were "kicking them out of the home." It will be that you are launching them like arrows into the world to have an impact in the world for good in everything that they do.

If you have done this properly, they will love you, respect you, and still look to you for advice. They will happily come home knowing that they have learned your life lessons, have applied them, and have been successful. That will give them great confidence knowing that their launching pad or foundation is built on rock. And it will give you great joy and hopefully wonderful Grandchildren!

Buying a home

When you consider buying your first home, buy something less than you can afford. In general, live below your means. You will be much happier. Many people live right on the edge, and get forced over the edge by life's events. Something always goes wrong. You need to give yourself some margin. It's so important, I'll say it again: Live below your means!

As a rule, you should never go into debt. Pay your credit cards off at the end of each month. When you pay the credit card interest for any reason, you are just giving money away. The one exception to going into debt is when you buy appreciating assets. Generally, that is a home, and most likely this will be the biggest investment you will ever make. Cars don't fall into this category; in case you are wondering! Pay cash for your automobiles, they depreciate quickly!

Again, do your homework when buying a home. Pay attention to location. Buy the smallest, least expensive home in the nicest area. It will appreciate the fastest. If you want to include land with your purchase buy a modest home with extra acreage that is zoned properly, so you can subdivide the land at a later time and make money on your land. Generally speaking, land also appreciates in value.

When financing a home, look at the interest rates you will pay. Sometimes it's best to finance for the longest period allowable. Sometimes it's best to finance for a shorter period of time if the interest rate is much less. For both cases, pay more than the minimum required on the loan and pay it off as quickly as you can. Being completely out of debt is a great feeling and takes financial pressure off your marriage.

Buying a home is one of the few things I would encourage you to go into debt for. It is an appreciating asset in most cases if you buy wisely.

Being a Success Professionally

> *There are no secrets to success. It is the result of preparation, hard work, and learning from failure.*
> *General Colin Powell,*
> *famous 4-Star Army General*

To be successful in business you must incorporate many of the Life Lessons in this book. All the ingredients are there. You just have to mix them together carefully and be flexible. Mike Tyson, the famous boxer, used to say, *"Everyone has a plan until they get punched in the face!"*

As I said about preparation, planning and execution, you have to have an initial idea or plan. It's good if the plan involves something you are passionate about.

Dedicate your business to the Lord and be generous with others as He blesses your efforts. Remember there are no short cuts. Developing and running a business means hard work……lots of it. You must be a good leader and take care of your people; they are the ones doing the work in the trenches. Be a servant leader. This means you meet the needs of those working for you.

Running a business or being successful in business requires perseverance. You must be flexible because circumstances change. Remember knowledge is power. Stay ahead of the curve for your area of expertise. Don't be afraid to ask questions and use what others have found to be successful. Celebrate small wins. There will be ups and downs in your adventure. Get ready for setbacks! There will be many of them, but each one will provide a learning opportunity. Be a life-long learner!

Keep cash in reserve and don't put all your eggs in one basket. There will be setbacks and failures along the way. Use and further your skills as a critical thinker. Be a problem solver. Bring people along who you can trust and add skill sets to your business that you can use that you lack. If someone is untrustworthy, don't be afraid to cut them loose. They made that decision, not you. Be open to creative financing. Be open to bartering. Be a good negotiator, but don't put your thumbs on the scale. Be honest.

People will remember how you treated them in business whether or not your negotiations led to a deal. Mark Twain wrote, "Twenty years from now you will be more disappointed by the things that you didn't do than by the ones you did do. So, throw off the bowlines. Sail away from the safe harbor. Catch the trade winds in your sails. Explore. Dream. Discover."

And the great Henry Ford, who started a business empire and revolutionized the world, once observed.

"Failure is simply the opportunity to begin again, this time more intelligently."

Conclusion

The Hard Truth

And the most important lesson I can leave you

If you remember nothing else from this book, understand the following Hard Truth discussion. Appropriating this "Hard Truth" will determine where you spend eternity, and further what kind of quality your life will be here on earth for the short time that God gives you breath. In John 10:10-11 Jesus said, *"The thief's purpose is to come to kill and destroy. I have come to give you life and that you might have it more abundantly. I am the Good Shepherd: the Good Shepherd sacrifices His life for the sheep."*

The intent in life that Jesus has for us is only good. But how do we get there? How can we experience this "abundant life"?

Belief and faith are summary words that describe broad concepts. Some people say that all you need to do to be "saved" is to believe and have faith. Do we need to have more understanding of these summary words? Think about it. Many non-Christians have faith and believe in a god. Take for instance Buddhists, Hindus, and Muslims. They are devout in their beliefs and their practice of religion. But remember, in Christianity we are talking about a special relationship....relationship with the One True God. And remember, these are not my ideas. These are the ideas of the God of Abraham and Isaac and Jacob of long ago.

So how can we have an accurate, critical understanding of the words believe and faith that leads to true salvation, or to spending your eternity in heaven with God? John the Baptist, who Jesus described as "the greatest man on earth" and actually preceded Jesus in life, said in the Book of Mark, 1:15, "The Kingdom of God is near. Repent and believe the Good News!"

According to the Bible, to receive forgiveness of sins and adoption into God's family, we must believe in God. In other words, to be "saved" and receive an invitation into Heaven for eternity, Christians must believe and embrace certain additional specific detailed beliefs and aspects of the Christian faith. Put another way, belief is not intellectual ascent. Belief is not saying, "Oh I believe that could be true". Belief is really believing certain facts laid out in the Bible. To biblically "believe" requires action. For example:

Jesus is Lord, Messiah, and Savior. If you don't believe each of these aspects of Jesus' identity and authority, you will not be "saved." Why? Because to understand who God is, you must come to Him in faith and have a basic understanding that He is the only true God; your Lord and Savior, the Messiah that the Jews have waited for thousands of years, yet rejected at His coming in Bethlehem.

Further, Jesus also stated that certain attitudes and behaviors would be visible to those who are being saved. For someone to believe in Jesus they would have to believe that He is the one true God, the way, the truth and the life. Jesus said this in the book of John, 14:6, "I am the way, the truth, and the life. No one can come to the Father except through me."

Did Jesus say that a person must "believe" or have "faith" to be saved? Yes, He did. But is that all He said that is required to be saved? No, it is not. What other things did He either state directly or teach as requirements necessary to be saved? He said that a man needs forgiveness of his sins. The only potential for forgiveness is the result of Jesus dying to pay our sin-debt and making forgiveness possible. This was necessary because there is no other way to obtain forgiveness for our sins. We cannot achieve it by our own efforts. You must repent to be forgiven. Repenting and committing to stop sinning require an initial decision (by you) to change your thinking and your actions. This requires effort and work. Remember, belief is action.

After we take the initial action repenting for our sins, we need to move on to making Jesus Lord of our lives. He is the boss, not us. To make Jesus the "Lord" of our lives means that we must surrender our lives to Jesus and His Lordship authority through humble obedience. This will require denying ourselves, taking up our crosses daily, and choosing Jesus' will, desires, and commands rather than doing what we want. If we are honest, this is difficult.

Jesus tells us this is difficult in the Book of Luke 9:23-26 where Jesus says to those who were following him around looking for another miracle: Then he said to the crowd, *"If any of you wants to be my follower, you must turn from your selfish ways, take up your cross daily, and follow me. If you try to hang on to your life, you will lose it. But if you give up your life for my sake, you will save it. And what do you benefit if you gain the whole world but are yourself lost or destroyed? If anyone is ashamed of me and my message, the Son of Man will be ashamed of that person when he returns in his glory and in the glory of the Father and the holy angels."*

Jesus is loving, but demanding....demanding, but fair. He wants all of us to love Him and to follow Him and to develop an intimate relationship with Him. He is a jealous God. He wants us to count the cost before we follow him. He doesn't want us to enter into a relationship with Him without knowing what to expect. He wants us to know being his sheep will cost everything, but it will result in Him giving you everything free of charge. He says, "Come to the table and eat freely". But you have to receive His gift of life. He will not impose it on you. You have a free will and He respects that completely. But you have to receive the gift.

Here are two examples of people in Scripture who understood the fundamental principle of surrendering to Jesus' Lordship authority from the book of Matthew, the 8th Chapter:

The Roman Centurion: When Jesus agreed to come to the Centurion's home to heal his servant, the Centurion stated, *"Lord, I am not worthy for You to come under my roof, but just say the word, and my servant will be healed. 9 For I also am a man under authority, with soldiers under me; and I say to this one, 'Go!' and he goes, and to another, 'Come!' and he comes, and to my slave, 'Do this!' and he does it." 10 Now when Jesus heard this, He marveled and said to those who were following, "Truly I say to you, I have not found such great faith with anyone in Israel."*

The persistent widow: A widow came to Jesus requesting, *"Have mercy on me, Lord, Son of David; my daughter is cruelly demon-possessed 24 But He answered and said, "I was sent only to the lost sheep of the house of Israel." 25 But she came and began to bow down before Him, saying, "Lord, help me!" 26 And He answered and said, "It is not good to take the children's bread and throw it to the dogs." 27 But she said, "Yes, Lord; but even the dogs feed on the crumbs which fall from their masters' table." 28 Then Jesus said to her, "O woman, your faith is great; it shall be done for you as you wish. And her daughter was healed at once. '*

There are a number of the other people for whom Jesus performed miracles. They understood Jesus' identity and subsequent authority and therefore received positive answers to their prayer requests. These individuals can be identified as people who referred to Jesus as the "Son of David", a prophetic identifier of the Messiah.

On the other hand, there are some individuals more like the "rich young ruler." Although he had belief, faith, and recognized Jesus' authority, he did not receive what he asked for, because he was not willing to obey Jesus by "selling all that he had and giving it to the poor." Jesus really didn't want him to sell all he had and give it to the poor. He was asking the rich young ruler what was more important in life: his wealth, or following the Messiah?

We are also warned not to make final judgments about other people. That's God's job. Don't entertain questions about any one person or group. Again, that is not our job to determine who is worthy and who is not....who will be in heaven and who will not. I've often heard that we might by surprised who we see in heaven.

In the First Book of Corinthians, 4:5, the Apostle Paul gives us some guidance in this area when he writes, "So don't make judgments about anyone ahead of time—before the Lord returns. For he will bring our darkest secrets to light and will reveal our private motives. Then God will give to each one whatever praise is due."

By way of encouragement, when we do receive the faith that Jesus freely offers us, we can be happy and confident when we come to God. The Apostle Paul tells us in Galatians, 3:12, *that "because of Christ and our faith in him, we can now come boldly and confidently into God's presence."* God longs to commune with us. He desires to live in us. He loves us with an everlasting love true to His character. He wants to spend quiet time with us. I once heard something that stuck with me: If you are feeling separated from God, guess who moved?

For different people, it's different things that keep them from God. For some it's pride, money and material possessions. Jesus says it's harder for a rich man to enter the Kingdom of Heaven than for a camel to pass through the eye of a needle. Money and material possessions have the ability to reduce our reliability on God. If God gives us riches, He gives them to us for a reason.

Some people may have had a bad experience in the church or with Christians in the past. But you can be assured of this: Whatever is most important to you, that is what Jesus wants you to be willing to give up. He wants a full commitment. And he knows what's in our hearts better than we do. He knows the number of hairs on our head. He knows us inside and out. He wants to have an intimate relationship with us, so that we can experience full joy in this life and the next! He only has our best interest at heart.

The bottom line is to have a relationship with Jesus, we have to repent of our sins, sincerely commit our lives to God and Jesus' Lordship authority over our lives, and be willing to obey whatever He commands us to do. That is the salvation message and discipleship message in a nutshell.

We can't obtain the gifts and opportunities of His Kingdom and His forgiveness through our own works and good deeds. Only Jesus can forgive us and give us those gifts and opportunities. He doesn't force His will on us. He respects our free will. He knocks on the door, but we are the only ones who can open the door and invite Him in.

In the Book of Revelation, 3:20, Jesus says, *"Behold, I stand at the door, and knock: if any man hears my voice, and open the door, I will come in to him, and will sup with him, and he with me."* He is always speaking to us. We must pray to have ears to listen. His heart's greatest desire is to have communion with us. Ultimately, it's our choice to open the door of our hearts to Him and receive all the gifts and opportunities that He has promised us. We must willingly receive The Gift.

The Apostle Paul describes this adventure as a race. The starting line begins with you surrendering your will to God's will. This requires belief and faith, not just a mental acknowledgment that there is a God, but truly acting on that knowledge. You must pray for God to become the Lord of your life and lead and direct you in His ways, not your ways. This requires you to count the cost of that decision. It is an acknowledgment on your part that you are no longer in charge. You are no longer your own god, but you are handing things over to Jesus.

The Apostle Paul reminds us in Ephesians, 5:17, that as we discern God's will and take our small steps in our faith journey: *"Don't act thoughtlessly, but understand what the Lord wants you to do."* Just before this in the same chapter, he writes in verse 10, *"Carefully determine what pleases the Lord."*

As we run our life's race, we must be thoughtful and exacting about our steps! They matter to you and to those around you. This requires faith, but remember faith is also a gift that God will give you. In the same way you don't jump off a building because you are aware and believe in the law of gravity, you must have faith that God has supernatural laws at work that control the spiritual realm. One of those laws and promises is that if you open the door in faith, He will come in and have relationship with you for as long as you desire. And I can tell you that once you have opened that door and tasted of the goodness of God, that you will not want to live any other way. In fact, at this point in my life, I'm not sure how people live without God. In the Book of Psalms, 34:8, David gives us this challenge, *"O taste and see that the LORD is good: blessed is the man that trusts in Him"*. This life has trials, but with Jesus walking beside you. You will have all the grace and strength to face each day that you need.

In this new relationship, God has obligations or promises that He has made since the beginning of time, but you also have responsibilities. Your responsibilities are to believe (with action) and have faith (living out your beliefs) and His responsibilities are to love you, to be there for you, and to ultimately raise you to new life for eternity when your days on this earth have run out; that is when your race is done.

I wrote a poem about four years ago to express my sincere love and adoration to God, my Savior. I have always felt very close to God.

O Sacred Heart, Most Blessed

O Sacred Heart, Most Blessed O Holy Lord I cry
To be forever near Thee With broken wings I fly
For Thy eternal blessings Sum up my full request
To linger in Thy presence And be forever blessed
Unworthy Lord I stammer To be forever Thine
Grant I may crossover And taste of heaven's wine
O Precious Rose of Sharon My heart yearns for Thy
    grace
Let mercy be abounding Reveal Thy smiling face
To Thee my Precious Faithful One I come on
    bended knee
Forgive my thoughtless ways O Lord I surrender
    all to Thee

Salvation is a "process" – A process that in my mind can be divided into three parts: 1. Repentance or doing a 180 turn on what doesn't match up with what God desires 2. Learning how to stay on the right path 3. And finally entering heaven!

Salvation Part I:
Repentance and the race begins

The first part is when you repent, believe, open the door and begin the race. That's when you are saved by grace. In the book of Ephesians, 2:8-10, the Apostle Paul describes it this way, *"God saved you by his grace when you believed. And you can't take credit for this; it is a gift from God. Salvation is not a reward for the good things we have done, so none of us can boast about it. For we are God's masterpiece. He has created us anew in Christ Jesus, so we can do the good things he planned for us long ago."*

Further, God wants us to do this in public. He wants us to not be afraid of acknowledging Him before others. In the Book of Romans, 10:9-10, the Apostle makes this message clear, *"If you confess with your mouth that Jesus is Lord and believe in your heart that God raised him from the dead, you will be saved. For it is by believing in your heart that you are made right with God, and it is by confessing with your mouth that you are saved."* You don't have to be a preacher, but you do have to tell someone of your conversion.

Unfortunately, there are some people who act like they believe, they might even "ask Jesus into their hearts," or have gone forward under pressure to receive an invitation to become a Christian, but then they go their own way. Again, God respects our free will. We can change our minds. We can put on an act. But God is not fooled, nor will He be mocked. This is a very sad situation, but that person has not been saved. They have gone through the motions, but they were not sincere. They did not want to surrender their will. Maybe, at first, they were sincere, but for some reason they changed their minds and chose the wrong road. There was no follow-through with their intent.

There was no evidence in their lives that they had a true conversion. In the Book of John, Jesus makes this very clear, in 14:24, *"Anyone who doesn't love me will not obey me. And remember, my words are not my own. What I am telling you is from the Father who sent me."* Jesus and God are One God. They always agree. They are always in unity. They are always One. But notice in this case for extreme emphasis, Jesus says, *"And remember, my words are not my own"*. Love and obedience are inextricably linked. There is no division. If you love Jesus, you will obey him and endeavor to follow His ways.

The Apostle Paul in the Book of Ephesians, 5:5-6, adds emphasis to this way of wrong living when he writes, "You can be sure that no immoral, impure, or greedy person will inherit the Kingdom of Christ and of God. For a greedy person is an idolater, worshiping the things of this world. Don't be fooled by those who try to excuse these sins, for the anger of God will fall on all who disobey him."

God will not be mocked. You can't fool God. You can't hide. God must be true to Himself. He sees everything for what it is. This is a tough concept, but these are not my words. These are God's words. In Psalms 146 David writes in verses 6 and 20, *"He made heaven and earth, the sea, and everything in them. He keeps his promise forever. The LORD protects all those who love him, but He destroys the wicked."* God promises to keep His sheep forever, but He also warns that God is true to His perfect character, His standards, and His principles that he has laid out very clearly for us, beginning with the Ten Commandments, which sadly you won't find taught in schools anymore.

If we have had a true conversion, we have nothing to worry about. If we have had a true conversion, there will be evidence that God is working in our lives. Our little tree will produce fruit in time. People will see a difference in our lives, however small. The Holy Spirit will work with us to change our old nature and our old ways into God's ways. We may stumble and fall, but we are moving in a new direction with a new Master. We are heading toward heaven. We are in preparation for heaven. Greg Lorie, an evangelic minister once said, "Heaven is a prepared place for a prepared people."

We are living in grace and forgiveness and we are not yielding to every temptation that comes our way. Make no mistake about it… we will fall into the ditch from time to time, but our desire, our aspiration, our yearning, or craving is to get out of the ditch and follow God again. It is not to go our own way. All we have to do is repent, ask for forgiveness and get back on the right road.

Salvation Part II:
Learning to stay on the right path

This second part of the salvation process of our life here on earth is learning daily to stay on the right road. We are exercising our free will to obey Jesus in our daily walk with Him. We are following His lead. We are working out our salvation with fear and trembling. In the Book of Philippians, 2:12, the Apostle Paul says, *"Wherefore, my beloved, as you have always obeyed, not as in my presence only, but now much more in my absence, work out your own salvation with fear and trembling."* You see that we are working. We are obeying. We are following in faith with deep reverence and respect for the Father of our salvation. We are a work in progress.

We are taking action on what we believe. We are acting out in faith. We are following God's laws because we believe God's laws to be true. This process takes a lifetime. This is where we are walking in faith. This is where we experience our ups and downs. This is where we learn to overcome. This is where we experience the mountain tops and the valleys. This is our new life in Christ. We still have challenges and trials, but it is very different than our old life, because we have a life-long friend, and that friend is Jesus. He is walking beside us, giving us direction through our mentors, friends, elders, our church and His word every day. We will reap what we have sown. As we walk with Jesus, we will learn how to sow good seed. We will develop a mature character and not be tossed about by every wave that comes our way. We, God's flock, are being prepared to be the Bride of Christ for the Wedding Feast of the Lamb that will take place in heaven. In fact, we have a reservation there.

The Apostle Paul writes in Colossians, Chapter 4 *"For we have heard of your faith in Christ Jesus and your love for all of God's people, which come from your confident hope of what God has reserved for you in heaven. You have had this expectation ever since you first heard the truth of the Good News."*

We will build on a solid foundation and it will be evident to those around us that we have a new Master who is giving us a new direction in life. Some fear asking God what He wants them to do with their life because they are afraid what He might ask them to do. But there is a more dangerous approach. That is, not asking God what He wants us to do with our lives in the first place.

Salvation Part III: Entering the Kingdom

The last part of the salvation process is the best of all. That is when we shed this earthly body and we are given a new body. We rise to life just as Jesus did. We are given what God has promised us, a new home with streets of gold. And the great news is there is room for everyone who wants to surrender and follow Jesus in obedience. It's a narrow road, but there's room for all!

In the book of John, the Apostle John tells us in 34:2-3, *"There is more than enough room in my Father's home. If this were not so, would I have told you that I am going to prepare a place for you? When everything is ready, I will come and get you, so that you will always be with me where I am."*

The Apostle John saw a vision of what heaven is like, and it was magnificent! The things that God has planned for His sheep you cannot even imagine! In the First Book of Corinthians, the Apostle Paul writes in 2:9, *"But as it is written, Eye hath not seen, nor ear heard, neither have entered into the heart of man, the things which God hath prepared for them that love him."*

I just can't imagine how stunning it will be! In his partial vision of heaven, the Apostle John describes heaven in the Book of Revelation, 21:21, this way, *"And the twelve gates were twelve pearls; each gate from a single pearl! And the street of the city was pure gold, as it were transparent glass."*

I love the song, *"I Can Only Imagine"* by the group Mercy Me. No doubt I will be on my face before God.

All our sadness from the circumstances and sin on earth will be gone! There will be no more crying and no more tears. All the trials of this life will be left in the dust. The race you have run with endurance and perseverance will be over. You will see Jesus clearly. Right now, because we live in earthen vessels, we can't see everything clearly. We don't know everything right now, but there will be a time when we do know God's entire plan and we will see the reasons for what we don't understand right now. In the Book of First Corinthians, 13:12, the Apostle Paul tells us, *"For now we see through a glass, darkly; but then face to face: now I know in part; but then shall I know even as also I am known."*

As I mentioned above, the Apostle John saw a glimpse of heaven. What a lucky guy! He saw a vision and recorded part of it in the Book of Revelation, 21:2 *"And I John saw the holy city, new Jerusalem, coming down from God out of heaven, prepared as a bride adorned for her husband."* We will receive and accept the invitation to the wedding supper of the Lamb. John saw this in his vision of heaven.

In Revelation, John writes in verse 19, *"And he saith unto me, Write, Blessed [are] they which are called unto the marriage supper of the Lamb. And he saith unto me, these are the true sayings of God."* How will all this play out? I have no idea, but I am developing an appetite, because I am sure that the Faithful God that I have entrusted my life to is the True God and true to His word....true to His character and His promises. He sets the rules and He keeps His promises to His people! He has in the past and He will in the future. It is who He is.......The Alpha and The Omega!

I repeat for emphasis: In the Book of Revelation, 3:20, Jesus says, *"Behold, I stand at the door, and knock: if any man hears my voice, and opens the door, I will come in to him, and will sup with him, and he with me."* He is always speaking to us. We must pray to have ears to listen. His greatest heart's desire is to have communion with us. But, ultimately, it's our choice to open the door of our hearts to Him and all the gifts and opportunities that He has promised for us in this life and the next.

I fervently pray that my children, my grandchildren, my family, my friends, and my enemies will receive this life-giving message and the important principles in this love letter from me. God bless you! I love you so, so much,

Dad & Grandpa

The End

TERMS OF USE

This is a copyrighted work and Bill Murray and his licensors reserve all rights in and to the work. Use of this work is subject to these terms. Except as permitted under the Copyright Act of 1976 and the right to store and retrieve one copy of the work, you may not decompile, disassemble, reverse engineer, reproduce, modify, create derivative works based upon, transmit, distribute, disseminate, sell, publish or sublicense the work or any part of it without Bill Murray's prior consent. You may use the work for your own noncommercial and personal use; any other use of the work is strictly prohibited. Your right to use the work may be terminated if you fail to comply with these terms.

THE WORK IS PROVIDED "AS IS." BILL MURRAY AND ITS LICENSORS MAKE NO GUARANTEES OR WARRANTIES AS TO THE ACCURACY, ADEQUACY OR COMPLETENESS OF OR RESULTS TO BE OBTAINED FROM USING THE WORK, INCLUDING ANY INFORMATION THAT CAN BE ACCESSED THROUGH THE WORK VIA HYPERLINK OR OTHERWISE, AND EXPRESSLY DISCLAIM ANY WARRANTY, EXPRESS OR IMPLIED,

INCLUDING BUT NOT LIMITED TO IMPLIED WARRANTIES OF MERCHANTABILITY OR FITNESS FOR A PARTICULAR PURPOSE.

Bill Murray and his licensors do not warrant or guarantee that the functions contained in the work will meet your requirements or that its operation will be uninterrupted or error free. Neither Bill Murray nor his licensors shall be liable to you or anyone else for any inaccuracy, error or omission, regardless of cause, in the work or for any damages resulting therefrom. Bill Murray has no responsibility for the content of any information accessed through the work. Under no circumstances shall Bill Murray and/or his licensors be liable for any indirect, incidental, special, punitive, consequential or similar damages that result from the use of or inability to use the work, even if any of them has been advised of the possibility of such damages. This limitation of liability shall apply to any claim or cause whatsoever whether such claim or cause arises in contract, tort or otherwise.

Other novels on Amazon by Bill Murray

Bill Murray's entire career has been unconventional; he is unconventional; therefore, wouldn't you expect his retirement to be a little unconventional? Well, it will be. For the first half of his career, he held various positions flying planes. However, during the last half of his career he transitioned to acquisition and program management. Colonel Murray flew two thousand hours in the F-111D/F, F-16B/D, and C-130H. In Renegade Colonel, he recounts his experiences over the thirty years that he served in the United States Air Force. From his early years as an airman to his later years in director positions, Bill has had the experience of a lifetime. In the years to come, he wants his family to have a glimpse into his life. How many people have lived in Canada, England, and Spain, burned down a barn, burned down two houses, gone to the Air Force Academy, burned up a room at the Air Force Academy, played Division 1 collegiate football, wrestling and lacrosse, flown supersonic fighters, crashed a plane and survived, had cancer and survived, had children and survived? You get the idea. Renegade Colonel is a book of experiences, but also a book of philosophy and instruction. I'm sure you will enjoy his sense of humor, pranks, misfortunes, and outright luck, but you will also identify with his love of country, loyalty to his wife and family, and getting to know his unique faith journey!

www.ingramcontent.com/pod-product-compliance
Lightning Source LLC
Chambersburg PA
CBHW060320050426
42449CB00011B/2565